Crash Into Me

Crash Into Me

A Survivor's Search for Justice

Liz Seccuro

B L O O M S B U R Y

New York   Berlin   London   Sydney

Some of the names in this book have been changed to protect the privacy
of persons involved. Conversations have been re-created to the best of the
author's recollection. Court testimony has been copied directly from court
documents. Some minor spelling and punctuation changes have been allowed
for clarity and consistency.

Published by Bloomsbury USA, New York

All papers used by Bloomsbury USA are natural, recyclable products made from
wood grown in well-managed forests. The manufacturing processes conform to the
environmental regulations of the country of origin.

LIBRARY OF CONGRESS CATALOGING-IN-PUBLICATION DATA

Seccuro, Liz.
    Crash into me : a survivor's search for justice / Liz Seccuro.—1st U.S. ed.
        p.   cm.
    ISBN 978-1-59691-585-5 (hardcover : alk. paper)
    1. Seccuro, Liz.   2. Rape victims—United States—Biography.
3. Rape—United States—Case studies.   I. Title.
    HV6561.S43 2011
    364.15'32092—dc22
    [B]
                                                                                2010020864

First U.S. Edition 2011

10   9   8   7   6   5   4   3   2   1

Designed by Sara E. Stemen
Typeset by Westchester Book Group
Printed in the U.S.A. by Quad/Graphics, Fairfield, Pennsylvania

For Ava

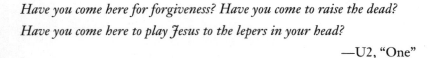

Have you come here for forgiveness? Have you come to raise the dead?
Have you come here to play Jesus to the lepers in your head?

—U2, "One"

Our lives begin to end the day we become silent about things that matter.

—Dr. Martin Luther King Jr.

Contents

CONTENTS

Prologue

As the freshman girl struggled on the filthy sheets, the stranger pounding into her, she looked to the left and saw a light outside the window. It was an ordinary streetlight that cast a blue-white glow on the revelers on the fraternity-lined street called Rugby Road. She screamed, but no one could hear her. Her breathing became shallow, caught in her throat. She realized now, covered in saliva, sweat, semen, and stale beer, that she might never leave this room. She wished for one thing: that her parents would find her, that they would learn what had happened to her and fight for her. She thought of her friends, her family, her life, and how happy it had been. She could let go. She could stop struggling. She stopped screaming and her arms and legs ceased their manic dance of defense. She said to herself, "It's all right. You can sleep now. It won't hurt anymore." She swirled into the safe and warm cloak of unconsciousness and quiet.

I know this girl. Somewhere inside me she is alive and not broken.

This is her story.

CHAPTER 1 *The Letter*

The morning of September 8, 2005, began like any other. Isn't it strange that the days that change your life immeasurably always seem to begin so ordinarily? Friends have talked about days in which they've experienced immense tragedy or great joy, and they remember how the day started with a decaffeinated latte, kisses, and an orange-juice normalcy that later seemed so bizarre in comparison. What is mundane and innocuous becomes alien.

My family—my husband, Mike, an investment banker, and our two-year-old daughter, Ava—was preparing for a much-needed three-week working vacation in East Hampton, where we had rented a house for the remainder of the month of September. I hadn't wanted to deal with all of those "summer people." We wanted peace, so we put off our getaway until after Labor Day.

We live in Greenwich, Connecticut, where life is usually easy and, frankly, filled with all of the material benefits that one could want, due to its high concentration of hedge fund operations and WASP pedigrees. The tree-lined main street, Greenwich Avenue, is home to some of the best shopping in the world; it's often called a New England Rodeo Drive. Mere minutes from town, the Back Country boasts massive estates owned by the scions of money,

both old and new, alongside the estates of members of the Holly-
wood elite—Ron Howard, Diana Ross, Mary Tyler Moore—who
seek out the quiet enclave as a respite from the rigors of the typical Los Angeles entertainment business life. Here there are no
paparazzi, no nightclubbing teen terrors. Perfectly highlighted
and buffed trophy wives brush shoulders with preppy girls and
young moms in the same boutiques and lunch spots. Convertible
Saabs and Jeeps grace the town parking lots alongside more flashy
cars such as Maseratis and Bentleys. There are no traffic lights in
Greenwich; just police officers who wave the cars and pedestrians
by. The old denizens of Greenwich felt traffic lights would be an
aesthetic blight on the famous "Avenue."

Mike and I moved here from New York City in 2004, when
Ava was just over a year old. I had attended high school in Rye,
New York, just five minutes away over the state line, so I was
quite familiar with the community. Mike fell in love with its
obvious seaside charms, great schools, and wonderful people,
and with its proximity to Mike's office and the city life we loved,
it felt like a perfect compromise. Still, sometimes it's nice to
get away from even the nicest suburb. That morning, in my
home office on the second floor, I furiously typed e-mails to
clients and vendors, letting them know I'd be out of town, but of
course, available via BlackBerry, laptop, and cell phone. I am an
event planner, so this is business as usual. I fill my weeks planning all manner of weddings, birthday parties, corporate events,
product launches, and children's parties. I've had famous clients
and clients who live next door. I have an intense passion for what
I do; unfortunately, that means that tearing me away from a

computer is a losing battle for anyone who tries to do so. Getting caught up in work, I tend to run a good half hour late to everything, and my own family vacation was no exception.

When I finally emerge from a steamy shower and jump into cargo pants and a tank top, I plunk a straw cowboy hat on my wet head as a final nod to the idea of vacation. Ava giggles uncontrollably at the unfamiliar sight of her vacation-mode mom. I double-check her diaper bag for the requisite supplies for the road, but then am drawn again to the monitor, just to check if the tiny e-mail envelope is blinking.

"Liz!" my husband yells up the stairs. "Seriously, are you ever going to be getting into the car?!" Mike is a man who is right on time, all the time. A dead ringer for the golfer Phil Mickelson, he is tightly wound and probably more in need of a break than anyone else I know. The Hamptons wouldn't have been his first choice—it's known as a playground of the East Coast elite, and Mike, a southerner, regards it with some reverse snobbery. Although he insists East Hampton is elitist, I suspect he loves the beaches in spite of himself. Still, he's taking this vacation to indulge me, and I love him for it.

"Just one more e-mail and I'm ready. Promise!" I trill in my sweetest spouse-appeasing voice down the golf-green carpeted stairs. Tappety-tap, I e-mail a client who is getting married in October about some last-minute decisions on lighting and menu that I want her to make in the next forty-eight hours. Ava is ready to go, towheaded and sweet, wearing a pink-and-white-checked dress and tiny white sandals, her silky hair in a ponytail. She is playing in my office and prattling on about the beach, my hat, and the movie for the car ride. I imagine that she is wondering about this mysterious concept of "vacation," since we have not taken one since she was fourteen weeks old. I turn to her, lift her off the ground, and spin her around, covering her tiny baby arms with kisses before setting her back down on my office floor. Flip-flops go on my feet and it is time to go.

Send. Save. Log off. Shut down. I scoop Ava up under my arm, jostle her onto my hip, and descend the stairs with a giant portfolio of color and fabric swatches and storyboards slung over the other shoulder. Mike gives me a wry look.

"Vacation, huh?" He stares at all the work I am schlepping, shakes his head, and gently guides me toward the front door before I can backtrack and double-check the stove, coffee maker, voice mails. "Let's go, honey. Seriously, come on." But as we fire up the car and queue up *Finding Nemo* for Ava, my obsessive-compulsive self takes over, yet again. We're pulling down the circular driveway when I blurt it out.

"Wait! I'll bet the mailman's been here. Get the mail, get the mail!"

"Oh, Jesus, Liz, why? It'll just be a bunch of Restoration Hardware catalogs and bills. Can't it wait?"

"No! You never know what's there. Please, honey? Then we can go."

Mike sighs, puts the car in park, and ambles over to the mailbox in his khakis and polo shirt. Ava and I start singing a song, while she kicks the back of my seat and tries to grab the back of my cowboy hat. I peer out and see Mike rifling through the mail, which does indeed look to be a massive haul of catalogs, bills, and a few birthday party invitations for Miss Ava—a baby socialite, lately. I feel sheepish. Of course, he was right. The white metal mailbox slaps shut with a rusty squeak. Mike's brow furrows a bit as he walks back toward the car. I give him my best movie-star smile in the hopes that he's not utterly through with me.

"Hey, you got a letter," he says with an odd look, sliding it across my legs.

I pick it up and flip it over. It's an actual snail-mail letter—a relic!

"Who writes letters anymore?" I ask as my eyes scan the post-mark.

Las Vegas. Funny, I know no one in Vegas. My eyes slide left to the return address, and the air is literally sucked out of my lungs. I struggle to catch just one cleansing breath, but it won't come. There on the return address sticker, so neatly positioned in the upper left corner, is his name: William Beebe.

The faintly feminine handwriting reads "Elizabeth Seccuro." How does he know my married name, and what's with "Elizabeth"? No one addresses me by my full name, except strangers and receptionists at doctors' offices.

My heart skips several beats, and when it starts up again, tears slide down my face.

William Beebe. My rapist.

"Honey? Honey? What is it? Who is this person? What's wrong? Talk, please talk to me. Talk, honey. Say something. What's happening?"

Mike is all over the place, looking wild-eyed and afraid. I must look as white as a sheet. I am subtly aware of rivulets of sweat escaping from under the silly cowboy hat. I start to hyperventilate and rummage in my handbag for a Xanax. Ava is in a tailspin; she can sense her mama is wrecked. I can distantly hear Mike try to calm her down. After what seems like an eternity, I flip the letter over. Out wafts the sickly scent of vanilla as I unfold a burgundy-bordered sheet of ivory paper. I blink, and then I read.

Sept. 4, 2005

Dear Elizabeth:

In October 1984 I harmed you. I can scarcely begin to understand the degree to which, in your eyes, my behavior has affected you in its wake. Still, I stand prepared to hear from you about just how, and in what ways you've been affected; and to begin to set right the wrong I've done, in any way you see fit.

He invites me to contact him at any time. He signs it, "Most Sincerely Yours, Will Beebe."

Out slides a shiny white business card with a red and blue rendering of the Statue of Liberty. It reads "Liberty Realty" and "William N. Beebe, Realtor," with his address, phone, cell, and e-mail address below. It flutters to my feet. Perhaps I am imagining this whole thing and it's some sick prank. Silently I hand the letter to my husband, who has calmed down for Ava's sake and mine. He reads it with no expression. He knows. He begins to nod slowly. I can hear the hum of the car engine again, and the sounds of *Nemo* drifting from the backseat. Normal sounds;

everyday sounds. Slowly, I exhale as the Xanax starts to take effect, but within a minute or two, the sobbing takes over, silently wracking my body. "Let's go," I say. Mike puts the car in gear, while looking at me intently as if to ask whether or not we should leave. I read his look and nod a silent "yes."

Pulling off down the circular driveway toward town and I-95 South, I cease crying and go completely silent. Ava falls asleep after thirty minutes and we turn off *Nemo*. I just sit and stare ahead at the road. I'm numb. It isn't until we reach Exit 72 in Manorville, Long Island, some three hours later that I come to life again. "Can you imagine this?" I ask Mike again and again.

"I know, sweetie, I know. It's terrible," he responds repeatedly.

"I mean, have you read this thing?" I continue to ask, incredulously.

We stop at a Starbucks. I pace back and forth outside on the patio, Ava on my hip. She's eating a cookie and I'm chugging a black iced tea and clutching the letter in a sweaty palm.

Mike encourages me to climb back into our car and we drive on to our rental in the Northwest Woods of East Hampton. I'm tired and dazed, but still very relieved to be away. "Away" for me now means something completely new. It means away from that mailbox. Away from the possibility that Beebe could show up in person at my home. Away is good, and we settle into a routine.

We spend most of the first week together, but Mike's job requires him to return to the city to work some days out of his office. I had hoped that he could stay the whole time, to protect me from . . . myself. Outwardly, I seem like a calm, tanned, and happy mom on vacation, but the demons swirling in my mind are slowly taking over, and memories I have tried to suppress for so many years are now as clear as the movie I rented last week. In fact, the memories are just like a movie on a constant loop. I see myself as a freshman at the University of Virginia in Charlottesville. Over and over, in slow motion, I see myself struggling under this stranger and I cannot for the life of me press the STOP button. That's the only way I know how to describe it.

When Mike is around during the week, we get a sitter and go to dinner, then walk the beach at Ditch Plains in Montauk for hours, snapping photographs or just simply touching fingers and breathing, looking at each other for a safe haven, a decision, something. The letter goes with me everywhere.

One night, yet another of insomnia (a legacy of the rape that has lasted for over twenty years), I go swimming at three A.M., blasting Coldplay's *X&Y* for an hour by the pool. Exhausted, I dry off, throw on pajamas, brush my teeth, and stumble into our bed, leaving the letter on the terrace dining table where we have been eating grilled fish and burgers each night. Sleeping fitfully, I am not aware that morning has arrived until I hear a yelp from the deck, where Mike is cleaning up from our Scrabble game the previous night. The humidity on Long Island is legendary and oppressive, and my letter is now soaked, the ink on the outside running in tiny streams down the envelope. I've read the letter countless times by now and it's committed to memory, but for whatever reason, I feel I have to preserve that piece of paper. We rush it inside like a trauma victim and blot it with dishtowels. It dries with a crunchy finish, but it's intact, and the spidery hand-writing is still clear.

From then on I'm even more vigilant, rarely allowing the let-ter out of my sight. (When I go through snapshots now from that late-summer vacation, I see a photo of me in a bikini, with a pink crocodile bag in front of me, and, yep, that's the letter right on top.) I won't even go swimming in the ocean unless someone is watching the bag with the letter. This means that Mike and I have to take turns swimming with Ava, the three of us never playing in the surf together as a family. The letter goes out to dinner with us. I unfold it and surreptitiously read it in restroom stalls all over East Hampton, just to make sure it's still the same and hasn't morphed into something else. If you recite or read any-thing enough, it begins to lose meaning. I realize I am slowly—well, maybe quickly—losing my mind. But after thinking and stewing and not sleeping, I've made a decision: I am going to re-ply. I *need* to know he's actually in Las Vegas and not creeping outside my door. That's it. End of story.

I'm not sure Mike would support this decision, so I decide not to tell him until after I've done it. My rationalization is that this happened to me before meeting him and it is my right to handle the situation however I please. I don't feel guilt, just a sense of great purpose.

On September 19, 2005, after putting Ava to bed, I'm sitting with my legs dangling in the pool, staring at my shell-pink pedi-cure in the turquoise water. Puffing surreptitiously on a contra-band Marlboro Ultra Light (I quit years ago), I click out the e-mail on my BlackBerry with my thumbs.

SUBJECT: Your letter

Mr. Beebe: I am in receipt of your letter. Please tell me how you can live with yourself. Tell me why you did what you did to me. My life was terribly altered by the fact that you raped me and I want to know why you did it and why you are reaching out to me now. Why didn't you just confess to Dean Canevari? Every decision in my life has been colored by wanting to feel safe. Now I don't feel safe again. How can you live with yourself? What do you want from me? Do you know what kind of a mess I became?!

I don't sign it. I reason he'll know who it's from.

I look up at the trees, exhaling the pungent smoke. The backlight on my BlackBerry goes off and I cannot read my words. Panicked, I hit a button and they reappear.

After five minutes of swirling and splashing my legs around in the pool, I hit SEND.

The little checkmark, which means my mail has been sent, appears on the tiny screen.

Immediately, I regret my decision.

During the week, Mike is back in the city and Ava and I spend time together at the beach and the pool. She calls me Mama Dolphin in the pool and I try to impress her with some dolphin-style cavorting and diving. She thinks this is hilarious. I put her in the stroller and take her shopping in town. Retail therapy is a tried-and-true salve for me and I resurrect and polish off this talent with a vengeance. We go to Pomodoro's for pizza and spaghetti and read *Clam I Am* by Dr. Seuss almost every night. She loves it because she loves all things ocean.

"Mama—read the part about the ocean being gray!"

She's a sweet angel. I hate putting her down for the night because I am left to go downstairs to my room or to the pool with my questions, a BlackBerry, the letter, some fine Long Island wine, and no one to talk to. But I don't want to talk about it. Yet. I told Mike after sending the e-mail that I had replied for my own sense of security, and he just nodded, not pressing me further. But as we try to enjoy our vacation, I obsessively check the BlackBerry. My biggest fear is that my time here in East Hampton will end and I will return to Greenwich to find William Beebe inside the house, hiding in my broom closet, the classic bogeyman. Or, worse yet, standing on my front porch, looking pathetic and southern frat-boy hangdog, begging for forgiveness in person. It strikes me how little I know of this person and his motives, and this scares the shit out of me. I certainly knew his motives back then.

And then *it* arrives. I see the "new mail" envelope icon in shiny bright yellow, I see his name, and I click on it.

SUBJECT: How do I begin?

"Dear Liz," he opens. Liz? Now we're on nickname terms? When he addressed me as Elizabeth in the letter, it felt more safely distant, somehow, since I never use my formal name.

You asked me to write about how I lived w/ myself in the wake of this incident. So I will.

He describes the selfishness of his youth, a time when he rarely thought about the consequences of his actions, especially when he had been drinking.

I always felt a tremendous guilt for the ways in which I imagined my conduct had damaged you, and for years too the only solution seemed to be the bottle . . . This is to say that the way that I lived with myself was of course not really living at all.

He joined Alcoholics Anonymous. He wanted to right the wrongs in his past. It seems, reading his e-mail, that he regards his crime against me as just one more instance of collateral damage from the alcoholic life he has put behind him.

I gather from your response that you are indeed still quite angry, and you have every right to be. I can only hope that some good has come of this by your counseling other women, that they might be free of their own bondage to horrific memories.

He says he prays for me. He signs it "Will."

I study his words. He has no way of knowing about my work with other rape victims, unless he has been doing his research well. It is dead silent outdoors, and the only sound I can hear is the roar of the blood rushing to my brain.

Now I keep staring at the damn BlackBerry, carrying the device with me everywhere. I don't tell Mike that I've heard back from Beebe. I tell myself I don't want to alarm him or cast a pall over his vacation. But we've never kept secrets from each other before. I wish I could just delete his e-mail, but I can't bring myself to do it. More needs to be said, to be learned, to be explained. I need to e-mail Beebe back, but I don't know what to say. What I read is that he feels bad, but my brain also hears that he's an addict who may be unpredictable. I don't want to rock the boat.

The next day, Friday, it's cooler and rainy, not a beach day. Time for a mundane trip to the grocery store in East Hampton. I tell myself to leave my BlackBerry at home. But then the phone rings with a Connecticut area code identifier. For a moment, the thought crosses my mind that it's Beebe, calling from outside my home. I answer it. It's Peter from Polpo, a restaurant in Greenwich. Of course. I've been calling him daily about the menu for a dinner I'm planning for a client in October, a few short weeks away.

That night, I e-mail Beebe back. Since he didn't reply directly to this e-mail later, my own words weren't archived, but I remember the questions I had and what I told him about myself.

Mr. Beebe: Why did you drop out of school? What do you do for a living? Are you married? Does your wife know what you did? Do you have daughters? Tell me who you are. My life was a living hell after the rape. Despite early promise, I barely scraped by in college to graduate. Shortly after graduating, I married a selfish, arrogant man who also went to UVA, born

15

to incredible wealth and intelligence, who wasted his life on neediness. Because of you, I married that person. Thinking I would be safe, thinking I needed marriage so early. You sound like him, although he would never have raped me.

I want to know who this man is. Almost twenty-four anxious hours later, my BlackBerry buzzes and I see his e-mail address. I am scared of him and his words. I am worried for my wonderful family and my mind. I am trying to figure this person out through nothing more than words on a device. The red light keeps beckoning, so I take a deep breath and click on the little yellow envelope.

SUBJECT: What happened . . .

In his e-mail, he continues to refer to the rape only as "the incident." He writes that he was disgusted by himself after the fact, but didn't realize the enormity of the "problem" he'd caused until he spoke with the dean of students, Robert Canevari.

He told me of the gravity of the situation from your point of view as he understood it, and from the U's point of view regarding possible judicial proceedings.

Beebe worried, too, about sullying the reputation of his fraternity. "It was," he writes, "too much to bear," and he withdrew from the university within days. (I learned later that his departure wasn't as immediate as he remembered.) He went to rehab in Arizona, a treatment program recommended by a prep school drinking buddy. He emerged, he relapsed. He was in and out of AA for nine years before taking what was (he hoped) his last drink.

He has no wife, no children.

I have always secretly felt, consciously and unconsciously as though I didn't deserve true unity w/ another woman after what I did to you.

Good God. "True unity"? I feel sick.

Once again, he speaks mainly about himself and not the effect he had on me. I don't know him, and I can't trust him drunk or sober. "I get it! Alcoholism!" I yell out loud. "So what? That doesn't give you an excuse! Why did you choose to rape me? Why are you contacting me now?" I fire off another e-mail, insisting on more answers.

A few days later I am stricken with a particularly acute stomach virus, head cold, yeast infection, and body aches all at once. Mike, in the dark about my continued correspondence, has no idea what is going on with me and takes me to the Wainscott Medical Clinic to be seen by a doctor. The doctor isn't sure what's going on, either. He takes blood, runs a pregnancy test (negative), and finally sends me home with antibiotics and sleep aids. I do not tell him about the letter. (If I had, I'm sure he would have sent me straight to a therapist.) Although I am falling apart, we try to enjoy the last few days of our vacation. We take long walks on the beach and collect pieces of beach glass we find shimmering in the sun. Ava especially loves helping to cull these little gems from the sand.

We have been home for a few days, and I have been lulled into the routine of work, laundry, and preparing for the start of preschool for Ava, when Beebe e-mails a response to my last round of questions. I have asked him about his talks with the university officials, whether or not he was aware of the rape epidemic on campus, and if he had happened to see an interview in the college newspaper, the *University Journal*, shortly after his attack on me, with an anonymous victim, speaking about her horrific rape. That was me, working with college journalists to bring some awareness to a grassroots cause.

SUBJECT: More answers I hope will be useful . . .

Hi Liz,

From what little I remember of Dean Canevari's talk w/ me, I don't recall any words from him one way or the other about dismissal from UVA.

He just knew, he says, that he had to leave. He reiterates that he now has "no excuses, no defense." He wants to understand my hurt more fully.

What's hard is, pray and ask direction though I have, and continue to do . . . I just sense such inadequacy to the task.

As if he expects it to be simple. "I'm sorry." And "It's all okay now."

He tells me more about life after leaving school. Back home with his parents after rehab, then back to Charlottesville, where he delivered pizza for three years. He didn't see my story in the press, but he saw others.

Perhaps you started something that no one else had the courage to do before. I like to believe that about you.

And why is he contacting me now? He quotes to me steps 8 and 9 of the AA program. Step 8: "[We] made a list of all persons we had harmed, and became willing to make amends to them all." Step 9: "[We] made direct amends to such people, wherever possible, except when to do so would injure them or others."

In 1993, he was sober, he had a sponsor. He wanted to reach out to me, but his sponsor told him it was not time yet, that it could dredge up old pain, that I might not be "ready to receive the approach." Of course, his sponsor was right about the pain, but he was wrong that it was just a matter of time.

In 1998, a new sponsor told Beebe to pray about the matter, and to start looking for me. Now living in Las Vegas, he has been in touch with a woman in AA in Los Angeles. She experienced an "incident" like mine in her life, and he is currently consulting her on every move with me. When his sponsor told him to look for me, he went through the UVA Alumni Office. They gave him my old address in another city, so his letter was sent back. Later, files updated, he got an address in New York, but that letter was also returned.

It sinks in that he has been hunting me down for years—and with the help of the university. This is the last straw—a further violation by him and by the university that never protected or defended me. Sitting on my porch in the fall twilight, I smoke and drink wine as Ava sleeps upstairs in her nursery. I vow not to write back ever again, and decide I must speak to the current university brass about what happened to me, so they will take a good look at their current sexual assault policies, as well as to dig up the files about my attack. But that's not enough to calm me. I creep into my kitchen and grab a knife. I hold it to myself on the chilly porch, alert, a sentinel, afraid and empowered all at once. I don't believe I'd know how to use it, but the blade feels comfortable in my hand. Sitting here, I realize the extent of my fear, and the lengths I would go to protect myself and my family, and I understand that I *have* to write him back, if only to ascertain if he really *is* in Las Vegas and not hiding in my bushes, lying in wait to attack again. And I have so many more questions that demand answers.

SUBJECT: Therapy

Dear Mr. Beebe:

Part of my therapy in putting this behind me, now that it is currently very much at the forefront of my consciousness, is to get a truer sense of what happened to me that night, as I have most of the details burned into my brain. To that point,

I need to know (and please, if you have any decency, you will tell me, as I do have memory of it, but I need confirmation) the following:

Were you my only attacker? I recall other people in the room. Were they merely spectators or participating?

I don't care how much or little you remember. But I clearly have an impression of this being either a gang rape or a "spectator sport" for the rushees. No names, please. But the nightmares for me must end. And I must know everything I can in order to heal and move forward.

The question of whether there were other attackers has been gnawing at me for twenty years. I know that the answer could be painful, but now that he has already reentered my happy life, how can I ignore it? I have to know.

Thanksgiving Day dawns cloudy and chilly in Connecticut, and I set about putting together a gorgeous feast for our family, including my parents and in-laws. Although I spend my professional life planning events for others, I still love hosting my own, and I'm happy in my spacious kitchen as I baste a turkey and make oyster and mortadella dressing, butternut squash lasagna, glazed carrots, asparagus with Hollandaise sauce, and mashed potatoes with homemade pan gravy. I turn out a chocolate-banana tart, apple pie, and cinnamon ice cream. But after my guests have arrived, between setting the table and arranging flowers, I creep upstairs like a thief to check my e-mail. It has been a while, but I feel a chill in my heart, padding up the stairs, my family happily gathered by the glowing fire in the living room. I just know, as those who hear the phone ring in the middle of the night sometimes simply know that something is amiss. And I am right. I have one new e-mail on this day of thanks and giving.

SUBJECT: More Answers

The night of the attack comes rushing back to me as I read his account of it. In his version of events, I passed out early in the evening, woke up around three A.M.

> I noticed you, we talked a while, how you were from Yonkers, how I'd been to Camp Dudley w/ your cousin, Bob Malafronte.

After "what seemed like hesitation," he says he "convinced" me to stay with him in his room instead of walking all the way home. He says he saw the "opportunity to have a good time with me." His roommate was away. Yes, there were other fraternity brothers milling in the hallway, but they were "not really involved."

He claims that we "started to make out" in his room. The door was closed and the house, quiet.

> There was no fight and it was all over in short order. When we awoke in the morning it was still chilly out, so i lent you my

jean jacket, and you walked home . . . There were no other men present. I was the only one.

Best to You and Yours This Thanksgiving,
Will

This scene of seduction, this romanticized version of events, is sickeningly removed from the reality that haunts me. Yes, some parts are foggy and I still have questions I hoped he could answer, but of course I remember the struggle, the terror, the pain. My blood boils with anger as I read. For the first time, I understand that, in part, he blames me for what happened. I furiously type back, oblivious to my family downstairs. I type as fast as my shaking fingers will allow.

SUBJECT: Re: More Answers

Dear Mr. Beebe:

This is completely different than my recollection. I was with a date, Jim Long, who the other brothers snatched away in order to smoke pot after giving us a "house tour." I kept looking for him as I was separated like a weak sheep. I had only had a beer or two and played foosball upon arriving at the party. I remember what I was wearing. The only person I knew in your house was Hudson Millard, who was an RA and friend to some of us. Some of the other, larger brothers physically picked me up and jammed me in your room. This, after fixing me a green drink which they called "The House Specialty" and repeatedly telling me that Jim was almost finished and ready to take me home. The drink disoriented me and made me very scared. I looked for Hud and could not find him for some time. Then I saw him. He was being carried into a room by some other brothers and locked in from the outside. With a padlock. My purse was in there.

I begged him to help me. I broke my toe kicking on his door and I realized I was in trouble. I was not passed out during most of your attack upon me.

I don't really understand your initial letter to me now. I thought you knew you had raped me and were trying to atone for it. I see now that your version is completely different. I remember every detail I possibly can, given the effects of whatever was in that drink given me.

I didn't walk home. I went to the ER. What exactly are you then atoning for? I don't have a cousin named Bob Malafronte, I can assure you of that. "We" did not wake up in the morning. I awoke wrapped naked in a bloody sheet while you were on your way out the door. As I recall, you were off to sell drugs, which I saw you take out of the top drawer of your dresser.

I do not understand any of this. I thought after all this time, you realized you had raped me and were apologizing. I trusted that your apology came from a good and honest place and I see this is not the case.

I send, and stumble back downstairs, to wrap myself in the comfort of the family gathering.

I wait three agonizing days for his reply, and, when I get it, it is only full of more half-truths. I have allowed the correspondence to go this far in order to finally make sense of the crime, and now I feel utterly dejected as I read his words. Is he talking about the same crime?

Dear Liz,

From what you write, I simply do not know what more I can tell you . . . I am sincere in my recollection, though it may not be the whole truth of what happened to you that night.

He writes that he was drunk, of course, but he doesn't think so drunk as to not remember. He assures me that he was not selling drugs—he could only afford small amounts for his own use. He is confused that Bob Malafronte is not my cousin. I was from Yonkers, Bob was from nearby Bronxville.

Also he is a natural blonde, as I recall also you are.

That phrase, "natural blonde," sets my eyes on fire.
He says he is "alarmed" by what I said happened to me, but that he believes what I said.

My lady friend in CA has asked that I ask God in prayer to reveal any facts as yet consciously unknown to me.

What I did to you, I did upon Matt's bed. Only the street light afforded any vision.

This is torture. But I can't let this e-mail be the last word. I want to let him know how much is clear to me all these years later. I know it is not helping anybody, especially not my family. Shamefully, I haven't discussed with my husband the ongoing correspondence since we returned from the Hamptons, and he hasn't asked. Can't he tell something is wrong? He definitely looks at me with concern. Since he hasn't told me to stop, I rationalize I can keep going, get more information. But he can't tell me to stop something he does not even know is happening.

Dear Mr. Beebe:

To answer your questions . . .

1) I had never seen or used drugs before in my life, so perhaps the drugs you had on you that morning were just for personal use. I am recalling something you said.
2) I did know of a Brooke Malafronte from home. Bob is not my cousin. As I was sober, I don't know how this translated. Brooke was a friend of a friend.
3) Jim Long was a dorm mate of mine, who was rushing your house. He asked me to be his date and I did not want to go. He desperately wanted to belong. He was sweet and funny and from Nashville. The other brothers upstairs took him away from me when I wanted to go home. I was lost and

alone, waiting for him. These brothers then pretty much delivered me to you. He never pledged the house.

4) I could show anyone the room I was raped in. It is the room you describe. On the bed you described as Matt's. I was moved to the sofa afterwards and wrapped in a sheet, where I awoke, bruised and bloody. I don't know how much you weigh, but I was about 5'6" and 115 lbs. at the time, which explains my injuries.

5) I have no opinion about Hudson Millard. I remember he couldn't save me or help me and I tried desperately to get to him.

I have a million other details, but you will understand if I want to keep them to myself. I want to [e]ffect change at the University and by sharing these things with you, the perpetrator, it may give them power to squelch my cause.

I simply suppose I do not know why we are addressing this now, except for the fact that it's part of your recovery and I cannot fault you for working on yourself. I think in recovery they don't really teach you about how your admission now causes turbulence in the victim/survivor's life. From my discussions with people in the program, I hear that addicts on your "step" just want forgiveness, neatly tied up in a bow. Know this: you and I will never be friends. I forgave you long ago. But I don't wish to keep delving into this, and now, I have no choice. I did not get to choose being raped and having my virginity taken from me so brutally. Now, I don't get to choose having this wound reopened. Everything is on your terms. I have a small child who needs me to be happy and calm and serene and this is not really going well for me. I am angry that your account is so very different than mine, which is burned into my memory as if it happened yesterday. But, then again, you were a heavy user at that time and I will not trust your account and [will] stay true to my own. I was a mere child of 17, but not stupid. And, I was rather sober.

Nor do they prepare you for the consequences, if any. This is very difficult for me. I feel raped and betrayed a second time. I have the most difficulty in your careful choice of words— there's a whole lot of PR spin, or so it seems. "Harm," "what I did to you," et al. don't really feel like coming clean to me. I suppose it's a difficult word to utter or even write, for you.

There. It is done. I have told him he's forgiven, which he is, and I have the feeling that's all he's really after. He doesn't want to know about me, who I am, who I was, who I have become because of and despite what he did to me. I wish I could better express how hurtful and frightening it is to hear from him, and tell him how painfully wrong he is about what happened.

I crawl into bed beside my husband, where I begin to cry. I tell him everything about the e-mails. Mike props himself up on one elbow, stares intently at me, his expression changing from sympathy to anger to fear in the time it takes for me to sputter out what is happening. He holds me and breathes with me. I look up at him and see tears in his eyes. Beebe has hurt him as well.

Once Mike falls asleep, I get out of bed and pace, unable to sleep, as usual. I have a hunch Beebe knows that we are at an impasse and that he is doing more harm than good. I step into my office, not an hour later that November night.

He has fired back.

Dear Liz,

I want to make clear that I'm not intentionally minimizing the fact of having raped you. I did. And I understand how our now differing accounts have evoked an angry conflict within you.

He says he doesn't know what more to say. He takes full responsibility, and is not trying to convince me of anything.

It seems that I'm actually doing more harm than good, which is not what I want to do. This wall in our dialogue saddens me. I hope it is only temporary . . . If you have any further suggestions, please let me know.

Best to You Always,
Will

I feel validation, but also deep pain. I have lost all desire to find out who this person is, and if I can't trust his version of events, I can't trust anything he says. I am broken. In this moment I do not know what the future will hold, nor how long the road ahead will be.

CHAPTER 2 *High Ambitions*

When I headed off to the University of Virginia in 1984, I am certain there was no more excited student in my matriculating class than I. The valedictorian of my all-Catholic girls' school, I had been accepted to several good schools. My parents were extremely proud of me: I was going to be the first in my family to attend college. The University of Virginia had not been my parents' first choice, since it was far away from our home in New York. I had never even seen the campus. But I had decided that I wanted to be a writer, and Virginia's English Department was ranked number one in the country at that time. Besides, I reasoned that it was the most practical option, since as a state school it was one of the less expensive choices. As it was, I waitressed all summer at a local country club to make extra money.

I had had a happy childhood. I was born to a Long Island teenager on December 23, 1966, but was given up for adoption to the New York Foundling Hospital by my birth mother, a student at New York University. My birth father was married to another woman, and this girl wasn't ready to have a child on her own. I was adopted by my parents, Barbara and Bob Schimpf, four days shy of my first birthday. They brought me home as an early Christmas gift to themselves, and I got a new birth certificate: I was named Elizabeth Anne Schimpf.

My family was modest in means, but rich in personality. We lived in an airy, sprawling apartment in the Fleetwood section of Mount Vernon, New York, in Westchester County, a heavily Italian American blue-collar bedroom community of New York City. My dad was a transit worker with the MTA, first as a bus driver, then a dispatcher, then as a major accident investigator. He was a self-made man and had worked since he was a child, when he sold peanuts at Yankee Stadium; his mother and grandmother laundered the players' uniforms. My mom was beautiful and stylish, with a sarcastic and biting wit. As the eldest of four children raised in the Riverdale section of the Bronx, she had been largely responsible for raising her younger siblings, for my grandmother was agoraphobic and an alcoholic. My mother never drank, although she did work—ironically, as an executive assistant at the Seagram Company.

My early years are a blur of good memories—summer trips to the Jersey Shore, vacations at Disney World in Florida, parties at my parents' house and their friends' houses where the kids would all fall asleep in piles of coats while our parents danced the nights away in double-knit polyester bell bottoms and jumpsuits. (This may have been the seed of my career as an event planner, as I was pressed into service to pass hors d'oeuvres at my parents' parties.) On nights when my parents left me with trusted babysitters, I would beg them to let me stay up late, so I could practice the dance moves from *Dance Fever* and *Solid Gold*, both big hits on television at the time, the era of disco. I was already taking dance lessons by then, too. When I was three years old, a doctor had noticed unevenness in my gait and a certain clumsiness, so he literally prescribed ballet lessons.

I eventually became more serious about dance, practicing every day after school and on Saturdays. Dance gave me a great deal of confidence. Always a fairly shy child, through ballet I learned to hold my head high. There were gorgeous costumes, makeup, flowers at performances, and curtsies at curtain calls. I made great friends, and backstage we would giggle until we cried and tell each other ghost stories in the dark dressing rooms. And, most important, I was good at dance. I had "the line," as the late ballet master George Balanchine would say: that alignment of the neck, the spine, the legs, the turnout of the hips, even the hands and toes, that was everything in dance. I pushed myself extra hard, trying to develop perfect technique to go along with the perfect line. When I was thirteen, my teacher recommended me for a summer of study at the Bolshoi Ballet in Moscow. The Bolshoi was the best company on earth. But soon after preparations were made, my trip was canceled. The United States was boycotting the 1980 Moscow Olympics, and it was considered too dangerous for me as an American to go to Moscow. This was a great disappointment. I started to lose my interest in dance, which now seemed like less of a dream and more of a chore. I had hit puberty, and I began to gain two or three pounds every few months. A knee injury sidelined me at fourteen. I knew I would never become a professional ballerina, and I quit altogether.

In high school, I turned the focus I had given to ballet to schoolwork and socializing. I dated a bit, but not seriously. I was a virgin, which was not uncommon in my set of friends. We were at Catholic school and took our religion seriously, believing for the most part that sex was best saved for marriage, or at the very least for someone we truly loved. Mostly, I spent time with my girl friends, and at our small school, we were a close-knit group. I was a straight-A student, played the lead in many school plays, and was a member of the student council, swim team, math club, yearbook staff, and cheerleading squad. I also became heavily involved in public speaking. Like dance, it was a way to express myself. I became state champion one year and a nationally ranked speaker in many categories, including Original Speech, Dramatic Interpretation, and Debate.

I had worked hard to get into college, and I was thrilled about going to UVA. Ever the perfectionist, I made multiple checklists as I readied myself for the trip down to Charlottesville, going through them with military precision. It was a hot Sunday in August when I crammed into the family car with my parents and most of my old and new belongings to head south. My best friend, Meg, was going to Trinity College in Washington, D.C., and was leaving at the same time, so our parents drove the same approximate speed. We spent that night at a hotel in the District to say good-bye to Meg, after which my parents and I journeyed on to Charlottesville. I felt good knowing that although I would be far from home, Meg would only be a two-and-a-half-hour drive away, if I needed her.

When I finally did arrive at my new home, I was struck by all the gorgeous red and white Georgian brick buildings, the expanses of greenery both on campus and off, the wildflowers and the vistas of the mountains in the distance. There were so many attractive and tanned students and families running about downtown that it seemed the small town would just burst from all of the action. I was excited about all of the new people to meet and classes to take. Once there and checked into our hotel, my parents and I were able to take the college tour we had never taken and learn about the university beyond the glossy brochure.

The University of Virginia, arguably one of the finest public universities in the United States, is in Charlottesville, Virginia, nestled in the foothills of the beautiful Blue Ridge Mountains. Chartered by Thomas Jefferson in 1819, it opened six years later. It is referred to as Jefferson's "Academical Village," a term he coined himself, envisioning a private, sequestered village where students and teachers would live together surrounded by beauty. The centerpiece of the university is the Rotunda, the original academic headquarters that sits at the head of the Lawn, a vast expanse of green that serves as the jewel of the university's physical plant. (The Rotunda you see today is a replica, as the original was destroyed in a fire in 1895.)

The great Lawn is lined by ten Pavilions, and a professor from each area of study lives with his or her family in that place of honor. The Pavilion Gardens, which echo the Georgian architectural style, are frequent gathering spots for parties and events for students and professors alike. I think this is how Mr. Jefferson would have wanted it.

Another legacy from Mr. Jefferson, and a big reason the university appealed to me, is its Honor Code. Under the single sanction Honor Code, those found lying, cheating, or stealing at the university are brought before the Honor Committee and, if found guilty by a trial of their peers, are expelled. There is no other punishment such as suspension or probation—expulsion is the only choice if you are found guilty. I served as an Honor Educator, and most of the cases I saw involved plagiarism and "over-the-shoulder" cheating. The Honor Code does not extend to more serious criminal offenses such as assault, rape, stalking, or murder. I liked that the Honor Code reinforced the idea of the Academical Village as a community of trust, where the goal of each individual who signed the pledge was to be not only a good student but an ethical person as well. Also impressive to me was the way students really ruled themselves and were responsible for their own successes and failures.

The university admitted only white male students as undergraduates until 1960, and women weren't fully admitted to all schools as undergraduates until 1970. At the time of my matriculation, almost 70 percent of students were "in state"—from Virginia. Out-of-states, like me, paid a much higher rate of tuition.

Some say that the University of Virginia, although a public institution, is elitist. Critics point to the special terminology used, which differs from most collegiate vernacular. At Virginia, there is no "campus"; the university has "Grounds." You are not a freshman or a sophomore; you are "first year," "second year," etc. You don't drink "beer"; you imbibe "the usual." And, God forbid you should refer to your fraternity as a "frat." There was a saying "If you call your fraternity a 'frat,' what do you call your country?" Crude, yes. But it marked what some would call the tradition of being a Wahoo. "Wahoo," or "'Hoo," is the name given to any student or alum of the university. (A Wahoo is also a fish that purportedly drinks three times its body weight, although the university denies any link, and the official name of our sporting teams is the Cavaliers.)

The unique character of the university was especially evident at the Cavaliers' football games. Where other schools have spectators cheering in jeans, sweatshirts, and face paint, we Wahoos would show up looking as though we were on our way to a garden party, which we usually were, after the games. Men wore sport coats and blue-and-orange-striped rep ties. For women, floral Laura Ashley dresses (at least in the mid-1980s) were considered de rigueur. Members of fraternities and sororities would all sit together in a show of Greek spirit and oneness. On game days, pledges would be sent to Scott Stadium to reserve whole sections for their houses.

The Foxfield Races, held in the fall and spring, were even bigger than football games for the university, and the whole city of Charlottesville. It was a non-issue whether or not you would attend. Foxfield, held on grounds in Albemarle County, is a respectable steeplechase meet on the horse circuit. We would break out our fanciest dresses and hats for the occasion, and the fraternity or sorority members with the biggest cars, trucks, or Jeeps would be elected to drive over and host the tailgate parties. Some houses would be decorated with blankets, silver candelabra, stemware, and flatware. You would see buffets of spiral hams, cheeses, fruit platters, biscuits, and serious desserts. People would work for weeks on their Foxfield tailgate presentations, with astoundingly professional results. Foxfield was serious business for horse aficionados, but students would joke about never seeing a horse, since drunken antics and fashion took center stage. One could see male students urinating on cars, girls vomiting in trash cans, and lots of hangovers and sunburn by day's end. Back then, the cops turned a blind eye to the underage drinking, but one needed only look at the long lines at the portable toilets to see how much students were imbibing.

Social life at the university revolved around Greek life. On any given Saturday or Sunday morning, one could walk down Rugby Road, the epicenter of the Greek revival mansions that housed the fraternities, and smell the stench of stale beer and bourbon, body odor, vomit, and fried food. In 1984 there were thirty-eight fraternities and sixteen sororities on Grounds. Those who were not Greek were known as GDIs, or "goddamn independents." For many, belonging to a house was the ultimate goal, and rush, the process by which new members were chosen for houses, was as complicated as any political campaign. Fraternity rush was held weeks after arrival on Grounds, and sorority rush was held at the beginning of the spring semester, in January. For the men it meant drinking Herculean amounts of alcohol while trying to find where to fit in—it also helped to know brothers from back home or from prep school, or to be active in a sport. For the girls, sorority rush was all about appearances—what you looked like and what you wore. Connections still mattered for the girls, but mostly connections to men. If your boyfriend belonged to one of the more desirable fraternities, then you could get the other girls invited to a mixer, thereby cementing your bid to a more desirable house. The rush process lasted weeks, until Bid Day, when representatives of each house would come to the dorms, envelopes in hand, to announce new members and kidnap them for a night of debauchery. Once you made it into a fraternity or a sorority, you were a pledge, which signified the time period before one was formally initiated as a brother or sister. Pledging was hard work. Men would go through periods of sleep deprivation, or sleeping on cold, wet floors and doing the bidding of the older brothers. They would undergo drinking contests, and some houses were associated with rumors of pledges being branded, forced to fornicate with animals, and being stripped naked and tied to trees for entire nights. Some men would be kidnapped, taken to neighboring colleges, and made to find their way back to Charlottesville without any money or transportation. Girls had it slightly easier, but were still woken up in the middle of the night to attend parties at crazy hours, made to parade around Grounds with sanitary pads taped to their foreheads, charged with stealing items from fraternity houses, and drilled on all manner of sisterhood songs. The pledge traditions were extreme, and sometimes cruel, but no one ever complained or got into trouble. Pledges would do anything to conform and belong, and it seemed obvious that the university would have stepped in to stop it if anyone were actually harmed.

But it was also clear that the administration turned a blind eye to the sacred traditions of the Greek system. The lion's share of alumni support came from Greek alumni. Who would want to mess with that legacy?

My first few weeks at school were idyllic. Everything seemed wonderful and exciting, if a tad daunting. It had been hard to say good-bye to my parents, but college was a new adventure, not only for me, but for my family. My dorm, my new home, was "cinderblock chic." There was no central air conditioning to relieve us from the heat of the Shenandoah Valley in August. We had one communal bathroom on our floor, which housed about sixty girls, and it was in a constant state of mess given our schedules in those first frenzied weeks—trash cans overflowed, shaving cream dotted the tiles in the shower stalls, toilet paper was frequently in need of a refill and toothpaste scummed the basins. My roommate, a bruiser of a girl named Alice, was a soccer player who missed her boyfriend back home in Pittsburgh. We spent virtually no time together, as she was always at soccer practice when not in class. Weekends, she visited her boyfriend. This was a terrific arrangement for me, because it meant I basically had a room to myself. As an only child, that was all I had ever known.

By January, Alice had left for good, to get married. My friend Caroline, whose own roommate had gone home with psychological issues, moved in with me. By that time, I was glad for the camaraderie of a roommate.

At the beginning of the school year, going to class was a celebration in itself. We woke up early, got dressed up in filmy sundresses and sandals with gold shrimp earrings and pearls or add-a-bead-necklaces. (As the weather got colder, we transitioned to fresh jeans and furry Benetton sweaters, with leather flats.) After dressing, we would march to Newcomb Hall for breakfast. The dining hall breakfast spread consisted of coffee, muffins, eggs, bacon, grits, all manner of cold cereals, fruits and juices, waffles, French toast, and pancakes. We all sat at tables with our new dorm friends, and if we could not find a familiar face, we would take books and notebooks out of our Kenya bags and pretend to study until someone sat with us.

After a class or two, most students gathered at the Greek amphitheatre in the center of Grounds, mere steps from the fabled Lawn, to study and sunbathe. Tank-top straps would slide off slender shoulders, skirts would be hiked up to the knees, and baby oil would be applied. And in the early part of the semester, thick, creamy envelopes would be waiting for us back at the girls' dorms: formal invitations to fraternity houses each week to hear bands, enjoy a theme party, or imbibe cocktails. Clearly, these invitations were extended on the basis of our looks alone, determined largely from our photographs in the First Year Facebook, a printed freshman register that was a standard feature of college use before the online social networking site students rely on now. It was a curious time—the careful wardrobe planning, the ablutions, the hair and makeup. But so much seemed to depend on it at the start of college, when anything seemed possible.

Even now, every autumn, no matter where I am, I remember the beauty and the thrill of Virginia in the fall—the gorgeous Grounds and the impossibly crisp air. To stand in the shadow of the Rotunda under the golden trees of the Lawn was a near-perfect feeling. The Lawn in autumn is perhaps the most hopeful place in the world, and it is what I choose to think about when I remember the university.

CHAPTER 3 *Darkness on Madison Lane*

On Thursday, October 5, 1984, I was enjoying a relaxing evening at my dorm, joking with friends, studying and eating pizza ordered from College Inn, the venerable institution of red sauce Italian and gyros that was a staple of university students' diets. I needed to complete a great deal of reading for the following week. I was planning to declare an English major, so reading would be a big part of my college years. I was exhausted, but having a great time with friends, watching some get ready to go out, some gearing up to watch *Late Night with David Letterman* in the common area of the dorm. We lolled about in the carpeted hallways, me in mint green sweatpants and a navy T-shirt, in bare feet. It was a balmy evening with the promise of a chill in the air overnight. It was a typical Thursday night. Around ten P.M., one of my friends, Jim Long from Nashville, came bounding onto my floor in search of me.

"Hey, Liz!" he exclaimed in his joyous, deep southern twang. "Wanna go to a rush party with me? It's at Phi Psi, you know, the big house at the end of the Bowl! I've gotta have a date, you know!" It wasn't a romantic invitation—Jim was gay. I didn't want to go anywhere, much less a house I had never been to where

41

I wasn't sure if I would know anyone. Jim assured me that some other kids from our dorm were going as well. But I didn't want to go; I was already ensconced.

"Oh, hell no, Jim—look at me! I mean, I'm settled in for the night and I have tons of reading to get under my belt. I'm sure one of the other girls will go." I gestured down the long hallway, filled with girls studying, eating, or putting on makeup.

I was sympathetic—Jim was right that he needed a date. During rush season for the guys, any man who seemed gay had better bring a girl on his arm or risk being blackballed by any number of houses. There were a few gay-only houses, but many gays didn't want to join for fear of being stigmatized. This was the early 1980s, after all. It was important for many young men to be able to pass as straight, although to me, Jim was quite obviously gay. Having studied ballet for so many years, I had known openly gay instructors, and it was fine by me. But I understood how hard it could be, especially for a college freshman. And rush was already a stressful process. After much southern charm and cajoling on his part, I relented. Jim was a friend, and I wanted to help. I trotted off to the communal bathroom with my makeup basket to put myself together. Once I had carefully applied some mascara and lipstick, I padded back to my room and got dressed. I put on a long-sleeved cotton crew-neck sweater of aqua, pink, yellow, and white squares, a Guess denim skirt, and a pair of navy leather flats. A strand of pearls and matching earrings completed my ensemble, along with a navy blue reversible Bermuda bag with wooden handles, so popular among the preppy set, which held my student identification card, room key, lipstick, small comb, and a bit of cash. Folding my sweats neatly on my bed and stacking my work on my desk, I bid good-bye to my friends and headed to the party with Jim and a few of the others from my dorm, including a pretty blonde girl named Cricket and her date. As we walked down Rugby Road, the redolent scent of Virginia dirt commingled with the sickening odor of the gingko tree berries and the stale beer stench that permanently wafted down the street lined by fraternity houses.

The Phi Kappa Psi house was a massive Georgian pile of bricks on Madison Lane, off Rugby Road, standing directly across from the Rotunda. It was lit up like a Christmas tree, music was blaring, and we could see revelers gathered with cups of beer on the porch and dancing in the large rooms inside. The party was in full swing.

I recognized a casual friend, Hudson Millard, a fifth-year resident adviser, working the door that night. Short, dark-haired, and affable, he greeted us happily. "Hud" was known by the younger students as a responsible and respectable guy who was always there with a ready ear to listen or advice to give if we needed it. He waved our group in and we entered the main rooms of the first floor of Phi Psi. To the left, foosball and music, keg beer, and casual dancing were the main attractions. To the right, brothers and partygoers were gathered around a large round table playing quarters, the beer-drinking game, and a small staircase led up to the house kitchen. To the far left was a large, dark room filled with leather sofas and armchairs with composite photographs of the brothers hanging over the massive fireplace mantels. Here, some couples cuddled, oblivious to the din of revelers and blasting music. Still tired and feeling a bit self-conscious in such a big crowd, I tried to rally and get into the spirit of the party. We all approached one of the many kegs and Jim poured a beer for each of us into those large, red plastic cups that are still a fixture at college parties today. We tried to figure out who was a brother at the house. Those were the people Jim would need to talk to if he wanted to gain entry to the next round of parties and, eventually, the brotherhood itself.

Feeling awkward, we sipped on our beers and staked our claim on the foosball table. I set my red cup of beer down on the windowsill and lamely attempted a game or two with Jim and some of our friends, jamming the levers of the table. Clearly, foosball was not my best game.

At one point, a few of the brothers came up to introduce themselves as members of Phi Psi, and chatted with Jim about his rush ambitions. A couple of them asked if our group, which included Cricket and her friend, would enjoy a house tour, explaining that it was traditional during rush to show prospective members what the house looked like. We agreed and carefully climbed the grand staircase in a group to the second floor. That floor had a large living room, a rumpus room that was set with furniture, a bar, and some music blaring from a stereo. Revelers moved in and out of the room as the brothers showed us the common areas and some of the bedrooms, which clearly had recently been cleaned for such tours. The bedrooms were spacious, most decorated with Oriental rugs and bookshelves, some with the Confederate flag tacked to the ceiling. Jim seemed excited to be shown around and was chatting animatedly to the brothers who came and went. I simply stood next to him, smiling. I had an early class, and hoped this wouldn't take much longer. At one point, I realized I had emptied my red beer cup and I refilled it from a keg on that floor, trying to look busy and sociable.

Back in the main room on the second floor, a small group of brothers approached us.

"Hey, y'all want to go smoke some?" asked one.

Jim looked at me and shrugged his shoulders as if to say yes. I didn't know he smoked. Jim leaned in and said, "They have pot." Ohhhh . . . that kind of smoking.

I had never smoked marijuana in my life and didn't want to start that day, so I told Jim I'd be fine staying in the common room. I was tired, but didn't want to walk home alone. How long could it take to smoke pot? "Good luck," I said. He assured me that he would be back quickly.

I watched them amble down to another room, enter it, and close the door. So there I stood.

Hud Millard was in the room at this point, and I saw some people I knew from my dorm, so I felt comfortable. At a party this large, it was easy to lose track of the people I knew, so I decided to stay where I was. Aimlessly, I walked around the room and found a place to sit in the crowd, on a sofa near the bar. Two of the brothers behind the bar acknowledged me with a greeting and seemed to be checking me out. They looked identical in their rumpled preppy threads and puffed-out-chest bravado. I had zero interest, but I was bored and didn't want to seem rude. They seemed harmless.

"You waiting on a friend?" asked one.

"Yes . . . it's time for me to go home. He's in the back, smoking with some of your brothers."

"Well, cool. We made some punch. It's called the 'house special.' Would you like one?"

I hesitated. I still had the second beer on the floor next to me and didn't want to drink more. I was anxious to get home. But I didn't want to seem like a loser, either. I figured one more drink couldn't hurt. One of the men put a pale green drink in a small, clear plastic tumbler on the counter and pointed at it, gesturing for me to take it. I sipped at it. It was very tart, yet sweet and tasted citrusy, like lime candy. My other friends were coming and going, and I sat down again and chatted with some people who looked familiar. What happened from there is a blur, but I remember some of the events in clear resolution, as if it were a motion picture. The mystery cocktail began to affect me suddenly: I began to feel lightheaded, nauseated, and dizzy. I was sitting in the common area trying to keep it together, but the drink had taken its hold and I was blacking out, awake but unaware or unable to remember what was going on. I lost track of time and I was scared. I remember talking with Hud, and I became aware of a very tall, owlish young man trying to insinuate himself into the conversation with chuckles and brief remarks. He had a large head, dark hair, and eyeglasses, which lent him a studious but slightly sinister look. He was staring at me and began slowly inching his way closer. No one was paying that much attention to him. Soon, Hud excused himself and this odd man began talking to me in earnest.

"Hi, I'm Will. What's your name?"

"Liz," I said. I was scanning the room, deliberately looking disinterested. I was foggy and I really had no interest in this stranger. There was a weird vibe about him. I felt like Alice in Wonderland. Everything was in slow motion.

"Are you a first year?"

"Yes."

"First time at Phi Psi? I'm a brother here. I'm a second year English major."

"That's great." Of course, I wanted to be an English major as well—a shared interest—but I didn't feel like engaging with him.

He said he wanted to show me something. I was not interested. At this point, Hud returned and was visibly intoxicated, or perhaps under the influence of drugs. I was alarmed that in such a short time he had become so obviously impaired. Had he had the green drink, too? He was a responsible man and this did not seem at all characteristic. Another brother came and dragged him into a room, the room where I had put my Bermuda bag for safekeeping earlier. The brother stepped outside of the room, turned, and padlocked the door from the outside. How would Hud get out? Why would someone lock their friend inside a room? Nothing made sense, and I was getting nervous. The room was getting blurry and my limbs were not moving as they should. I felt like a marionette, and it was difficult to stand up on my own. It was most certainly time to head home. I desperately wanted to leave, but the thought hit me: "I can't walk home alone. I don't even think I can walk, period."

I tried to remain calm. Surely Jim would be back for me soon.

So I cooled my heels, trying to act normal. I inquired around the room about Jim's whereabouts, only to be told several times, in so many ways, "Oh, he'll be back soon. Just hang out here and he'll be back to walk you home." I sat and waited. My breathing felt shallow and a little panicky. What was in that drink?

Again, the tall man appeared at my side. Talking, leaning in, and whispering. Again, I shrugged him off, reiterating that I was waiting for my friend and that I would be going home soon, as I had an early class to attend. I shifted on the couch, twisting away and searching for someone, anyone that I knew. No one looked familiar. Then, he took me by the hand and lifted me off the couch.

The young man began to yank me toward a room, telling me he wanted to show me something.

"No. Really, I don't want to see whatever it is. I'm fine here. Let me go back." "No, you'll like it!" he insisted. Pulling. Dragging. In the room, he grabbed a slender volume covered in green fabric from a nearby table, sat in a chair, and pulled me onto his lap with his arms locked around my waist. As I struggled to get free, he began to read poetry to me, and then to lick the area behind my ear. I pulled away, repulsed. I had done nothing to indicate I was at all interested in this person. "Hey, let me go!" I said with a forced smile. But I was serious and more than a little frightened.

He tightened his grip on me and told me to relax, but I broke free and ran to the room where Hud was locked in. I pounded on that door, screaming with all my might and kicking the door. It seemed like I was at that door, scraping and kicking and screaming for hours. It may only have been a minute or two. One of the brothers from behind the bar came up to me and yelled at me to shut up. The music suddenly got louder in the room and my protests were drowned out. This brother was extraordinarily tall, wearing a plaid flannel shirt and a navy and orange Virginia baseball cap. He picked me up like a sack of autumn leaves, threw me over his shoulder, and shoved me back into the room, depositing me into the waiting arms of the poetry-reading weirdo. He gave a high five to another brother. I screamed.

The door was slammed shut loudly and the lights were cut. I swam in total blackness and could not stand on my own. Someone was holding me up and ripping my clothes off roughly, restraining me first by one arm, then the other. My sweater was stretched over my head, my skirt unzipped and roughly shoved down to the floor. My white cotton bra was unhooked and my matching white panties yanked down over my knees, which caused me to fall. I was wildly shaking my head and flailing. Horror washed over me. I had never been naked in front of anyone in my life. At that point, I was shoved roughly onto the bed. I could hear him unzip his pants as he covered my mouth with his hand, hissing "Bitch, shut up." He sat down on my thighs so that I couldn't move my legs and the pain was intense. I realized I was still wearing my shoes. I was able to bend my knees at an outward angle at one point and kick him in the back with my hard wooden soles. My assailant yelped in pain and moved farther down on my legs, sitting on my shins now to stop the assault of my kicks. Rubbing his hands over my breasts, he tried to fondle me as I twisted away from his grasp, batting his hands away as best I could. He quickly pinned down my arms with his forearm. Panicking,

I could hear myself panting and gasping for breath. I screamed again, but don't think any sound escaped my mouth.

The assailant was still fully clothed from the waist up, with his pants pulled down around his ankles, from what I could feel. I could feel his bare, sweaty thighs on me. He tried to force his penis inside me, but I was a virgin, and he was struggling. He took his hand and shoved it inside me. I screamed "No" repeatedly. My heart was racing and my mouth ran dry. He stank. He rammed himself inside me as he squeezed my arms and put all of his body weight on me. I turned my head swiftly back and forth to avoid his mouth. Looking out the window to my left, I could see revelers on Madison Lane under the blue-white glow of the street lamp. With each thrust, my head was slammed into the head- board or wall behind me; when I tried to lift my head, my cheek- bone was smashed into the same surface. He grunted on top of me as I tried to lock my legs together and fight him off. "Please, no," I begged. "Stop!"

Despite my screams, he held me down and thrust into me re- peatedly. I thought I was going to die in this filth. During the act, I heard doors opening and shutting and could see lights—maybe someone would help me. At one point, with horror, I sensed others in the room. I heard shouts and excited voices. But within a split second, my mind went dark again. All I could feel was some- thing warm and wet gushing between my legs. I tried to focus on thoughts of my family and of God. Then, with a wash of pain, I passed out.

In the dark hours of that night, I remember feeling movement around the room, and remember being jostled. Was I being moved? Was I being raped again? I could feel something underneath me and the sensation of dragging, but I could not open my eyes or speak. I have flashbacks of hearing a shower running and feeling water on my back. Cold tile under my face. Time standing still and me not being able to move.

There was a shout in the hallway, "Holy shit! What did you do to her?!" but I could not open my mouth. It was sealed shut with dried, scummy residue and the rest of me could not move. I don't know how long I lay there or how many people saw me. I heard a commotion somewhere on the floor with shuffling and yelling. The music started and stopped over and over. My body and brain swam down into a warm nest. I tried to lift my head at one point and I felt someone touching my face as I fell back into darkness.

Hours later, sunlight streamed through a window. I opened my eyes and assessed my situation. My mouth was almost glued shut with film. Where was I? I slowly became aware that I was in a room with a bed, two desks, and a loft bed above me. My eyes scanned to the right and left in the early-morning sun and I realized I was on a couch and that it was probably before seven A.M. My head hurt horribly; I raised one hand to the back of my head and felt a painful lump at the crown. I was wrapped in a dirty sheet. With horror, I looked down and saw the bloodstains from my thighs all the way down to my ankles. I began trying to peel the sheet off my body, but the blood was dried and brown and it felt like ripping a bandage from a scab.

Finally, I got free and shakily stood up, holding the sheet to my body. I steadied myself on the post to the loft bed, and crept over to the dresser. There was a pile of papers and mail on the top. "Will." The name jumped into my mind. Someone named Will. Sure enough, I saw his name in the papers. William Beebe. As I put the papers down, I heard footsteps behind me. I froze. There he stood, just as I remembered him. His face terrified me. This man was an evil man, I thought. This man had hurt me.

But his face smiled.

"Well, I hope I was a gentleman last night."

I said nothing. I tried to figure out how to escape.

"No? Hey, you'd better get out of here before someone sees you. Take a jacket if you want. It's chilly out there." His head jerked toward what I assumed was a closet door.

I couldn't move. How could he be speaking to me after the violence of the night before? I was still afraid of what he could do to me, so I stood stock-still as he gathered his things and packed his backpack. Out of the corner of my eye, I saw him take a plastic baggie that looked to be filled with a white powdery substance out of the top drawer of the dresser. I just stood with my head down, scared.

"Hey," he said loudly. I snapped my head up and looked him in the eye. With a stern look, he pointed his finger at me in warning. He kept that finger pointed at me for about twenty seconds. Then, he turned on his heel and left the room, clomping down the two flights of stairs. Why was *he* warning *me*? I heard the creak of the front door open and close. I did not breathe or move for at least three minutes. Stillness. No sounds.

I scrabbled on the floor in the sheet, like a desperate animal, looking for my clothing. By now, the full realization of what had happened was crashing into me. There was my skirt, there, my bra. Farther down the room, almost under the bed, was my sweater. Hastily, I put these things on. My hands flew to my neck and ears; my earrings and necklace were still on my body. I couldn't find my underpants, but I didn't want to stay to hunt for them any longer. Going to the closet, I grabbed a large denim jacket to wear outside. Then I found a piece of paper and a golf pencil on top of a desk. I wanted this animal to know that I knew what he had done. I would write a note and leave it on the bed, which was covered with bloodstains.

"If you ever want this jacket back, you can come to get it at Gwathmey, room 222. I won't be alone, so don't even think about trying to hurt me again." I had no idea why I was giving him my personal information, but I couldn't find the words I wanted, to match the gravity of the situation. I wanted to let him know by this note that I was not going to let him off the hook. I had no idea what else to do. I was disoriented and mortified, but I knew what had happened to me, and that it was serious.

I limped into the filthy, green-tiled bathroom, where there were three toilets in a row with no seats on them. Bright yellow urine stains spattered the rims of each one and the tile floor was also spotted with dried urine. One toilet was filled with unflushed feces. There was crusted vomit in a small plastic trash can under one of the sinks. I desperately had to go to the bathroom, but there was no toilet paper. I tried to squat, but my shaky legs gave out and I sat on the seatless toilet. When the flow finally came, it burned like fire as I let out an audible yelp and put my head in between my legs to keep from fainting. Standing up, my own urine dripped down my leg as I went to one of the sinks and turned on the cold spigot. As I looked up into the dirty mirror, I noticed blood on my lip and a small, lurid bruise forming on my cheekbone. I picked up a filthy hand towel, running it under the cold water. It reeked of mold, but I did not care as I ran the damp towel up and down my legs and thighs, scrubbing off the dried blood and urine. I even used it on my mouth, although the stench of the fetid thing overwhelmed me.

With my shoes in my hand, I ran out into the hall and leaned over the railing, looking down the dizzying spiral staircase. It occurred to me then that there was not one person in the entire house. It reeked of alcohol, sweat, and smoke, but I could hear nothing. This seemed odd in the early-morning hours after a large rush party. Where was everyone? Were they hiding? Lying in wait for me? My heart pounded so hard I could actually see my sweater moving. The doors to all of the rooms were shut, except for the room Hud had been locked in. There was no Hud, and my Bermuda bag was on the chair, right where I had left it. Where had he gone? The whole scene was eerie. I had to get out of there. I knew I had to do something to help myself, that I had to tell someone what had happened to me.

Because what happened to me had a name. An ugly name. It was called rape.

CHAPTER 4 *Sweeping It Under the Rug*

I hobbled silently down the staircase of Phi Kappa Psi. I went out to the front porch and down the wedding-cake steps onto Madison Lane. I blinked at the sun and automatically turned right, toward Rugby Road and my dorm. But then something in my brain whirred and clicked like a shutter of a camera lens and I turned around and went left instead, propelled on numb, sticky legs as I walked over to University Avenue, where I took another left and walked the entire Corner (a stretch of shops and eateries on University Avenue). It was about eight in the morning by now. Suddenly, I realized that I was still holding my navy leather flats, hanging from two crooked fingers. At first, I had not put on my shoes because I wanted no one to hear me creep down the stairs of the house. But now I saw that I couldn't put them on if I tried—my toe was too swollen from trying to kick down the locked bedroom door. As I walked I looked straight down, to avoid eye contact with anyone. I was walking in the opposite direction of any undergraduate classrooms, so it was unlikely I would be greeted by anyone I knew. I simply did not want to see anyone who might remember me, naked, at that party, any-one who had watched me being savagely violated. As the terrible assault flashed through my head, I became even more convinced in my horrifying sense that people had watched it happen. The shame was overwhelming. It was a sunny, crisp day—the same beautiful fall weather that had delighted me the day before. I tried to focus on the feeling of the sun on my face as I put one foot in front of the other. I willed myself to walk. Just walk.

At seventeen, I had had no experience with crime or with sex, but I knew that after something so unspeakably violent and horrible I needed to get to a hospital. In 1984, there were no cell phones—no easy way to call a friend to help me, or drive me. I just had to get to the hospital on my own. My bruises and bleeding felt acute and as I became more aware of my body, I noticed that it hurt when I tried to breathe deeply. My head and face throbbed, my vaginal area was burning, and my whole body felt tender and swollen.

At some point, I became aware of the pain on the soles of my feet. Realizing I was stepping on painful pebbles and bits of trash, I forced my shoes on to my swollen, throbbing feet for the rest of the long walk.

I walked through the sliding glass doors of University of Virginia Medical Center emergency room, scanned the lobby, and took a deep, painful breath. My legs were wobbly and shaky. I walked first to a water fountain and took a big drink, the water dribbling down my chin onto my sweater. Then, I straightened up and approached a desk, where I simply stood, not summoning anyone. I just stood there like a ghost. Finally, a middle-aged woman in scrubs came up and asked if I needed anything.

"I've been raped. I need to see someone. I think I am hurt," I said.

Immediately, she came around the desk and took me by the arm, walking me toward a bank of chairs.

"Honey, what did you say?"

"I've been raped," I repeated in a near whisper. "I don't feel well and I need to see a doctor." She led me quietly to a chair. She knelt down beside me, and asked me to tell her everything that had happened. In broken sentences, I told her. "Let me see what I can do for you," she said.

I sat in that chair for a long time, replaying not only the horror of the night before, but the sheer terror of William Beebe confronting me in his dark bedroom that morning. I stood up and got a pile of magazines to distract myself, but I couldn't read them. I kept looking up at the desk to see if someone was ready to see me. Every once in a while, I noticed one of the doctors, nurses, or EMTs looking at me. But I was left waiting.

After what seemed like hours, the kind nurse came back, bearing a Styrofoam cup of tea with milk in it. "Drink this," she told me. "It will help you feel better to drink something warm."

I accepted the tea gratefully, and she disappeared again. Again, I was left waiting. I was anxious, scared, and in pain, but I had never been to an ER before. It seemed that everyone else was waiting, too, that these things just took a long time. I sat quietly where I was told. Out the window, I saw the light changing, the day progressing.

At last, the kind nurse returned. I brightened as she came toward me, but her face looked sad.

"Sweetheart—here's what's going on. What you need to have done, we cannot do here."

I stared at her blankly.

"You need to have some tests done and we don't do that here. You need to go to a major city hospital—perhaps in Richmond or Washington, D.C. Can you do that?"

Could I do that? I didn't understand. This happened here in Charlottesville. What test was it that a doctor couldn't do at this world-class teaching hospital?

"I don't have a car, ma'am," I said. "And I don't have money to take a train. Why can't someone examine me here?"

"Honey, you need to have special exams done for a rape and we don't have those tests here. Do you have a friend who can take you?"

I just shook my head. I felt overwhelmed and completely alone. There was no way I could take the long trip right now to Richmond or D.C. I didn't even thank her. I just gathered my things and walked out the door. I wanted to go to my dorm, to be around friendly faces. Perhaps my resident adviser could help. My legs carried me gingerly to my dorm. I passed the bike racks and some students lolling on the grass in the chilly sun and opened the heavy front door with much effort. Once inside, I climbed the stairs, found my key in my bag, and entered my room. Alice was away in Pittsburgh for the weekend, as usual. My green sweatpants were folded neatly on the bed where I had left them. My stack of books and assignments was still on my desk. What now?

What now? I realized with shock that I was wearing William Beebe's denim jacket. I shrugged it off my body and crumpled it into a ball that I threw on the bottom of my small closet. What now? I peeled off my clothes, put them in a plastic grocery bag, and left them in the closet near the jacket. I wrapped my aching body in my pink bathrobe, grabbed my plastic container of toiletries and two towels, and headed for the bathroom down the hall.

I turned on the water in one of the more hidden shower stalls. When it became scalding hot, I climbed in and began to scrub myself vigorously with a washcloth and soap. I watched the rusty-brownish water swirl down the drain before realizing I was staring at my own blood draining off my body. My face stung when I lifted it to the spray. My lip was throbbing and I noticed fingerprint-sized bruises on my arms. Everything hurt—touching my vaginal and anal areas made me cry out in pain. I wanted him and his vile, nasty stench off me. OFF. I used my hands instead of a washcloth to gently clean my genital areas. I shampooed and conditioned my hair, and then I slid down and sat on the tile floor of the shower, letting the water pound over my head. I didn't cry. I just sat and soaked in the downpour.

Twisting my hair into a turban with one towel and wrapping the other around me, I approached the filthy sinks and brushed my teeth, purging any sticky residue of that drink or his saliva. I felt clean. So clean. When I finished, I folded my sore limbs back into my robe, padded back to my room, and crawled into my bed with my hair still in the towel. I lay still there for a while, before sitting up with sudden urgency. The hospital hadn't helped and

I still needed to tell someone. I grabbed the phone by my bedside and called my friend Caroline. "Hello?" It was late afternoon by now, and luckily she was back from class.

"Caro, it's Liz. I need you. There's been trouble."

I hung up before she could ask questions.

Shortly after, she burst into my room.

"What's wrong? What's the trouble?"

I told her the story of the whole horrible night, the frightening morning, and the long, frustrating day. I pointed to my closet to show her the jacket. Like me, she wasn't quite sure what we should do next, but she was deeply worried, even panicked. She squeezed my hand and told me she'd be right back.

Minutes later, there were about five or six people gathered in my room, a group of concerned dorm friends. I finally felt like I could safely relax, surrounded by people who cared.

I curled in the fetal position on my bed. People drifted in and out of the room, fetching Cokes, tea, water, asking what I needed. They spoke in hushed tones as I lay there, in pain. Someone brought some aspirin, which I gratefully accepted.

"Someone should get Jonathan," someone said. I heard footsteps running down the carpeted hallway. Jonathan was an upperclassman friend. He was dating a girl who lived on my hall and was sort of an informal adviser to many of us. He came into the room, bringing a clear sense of authority.

"Everyone give her some room!" he bellowed.

He sat on the bed and hugged me.

"What happened?" he asked.

I couldn't bring myself to tell the story again and I started to sob, great heaving, choking sobs. One of my friends gave him the short version. He hugged me so tightly that my already-bruised ribs hurt and he said, *"You stupid, stupid, girl.* Why don't they tell you never ever to go upstairs at one of those houses? Why?"

I went cold. He had called me stupid. This had happened to me because I was a "stupid" girl. Of course, Jonathan was primarily expressing his frustration with the university and its failure to give first years thorough safety briefings, its unwillingness to suggest that fraternity houses could be dangerous places, especially during rush. But this was the first suggestion that my actions had contributed to my brutal attack. This is how it begins, the cycle of self-blame and destruction.

I was shaking, but Jonathan just hugged me tighter and gave some orders around the room for more blankets, summoning people as needed while clearing others out. I was left with Jonathan and Caroline. Sleep was beginning to beckon and I drifted in and out until it was dark. Someone turned on a small desk lamp so I wouldn't be frightened and they stayed there with me all night. Tightly wrapped as I was in my robe, the sweat poured off me, but I could not have cared less. At one point, someone helped me to the bathroom, where I urinated for what seemed like the first time in ages. The burn felt like someone had poured acid on my genitalia and I actually screamed. Fresh blood began leaking out of me and I asked my friend to get me a sanitary pad to line my underwear. She assisted me back to my dorm room and I crawled back into bed and slept fitfully until dawn.

When I awoke, there were three people in my room and I was fuzzy and disoriented, unsure where I was. Every part of me that had hurt, hurt more. I was one big bruise, throbbing and tender. I was clutching a stuffed blue seahorse. Someone told me that Samira, the adorable grad student down the hall, had brought it for me and tucked it into my arms in the middle of the night. I will never forget that. Still awake, I began panicking—what was I to do? Who knew about this? What was being said? Jonathan asked, "Is there someone we can call for you?"

"Meg," I said, thinking of my best friend from high school. "I need to call Meg. She's at Trinity in D.C. I need her here."

Flipping through my little address book, I found her number and dialed it. Meg answered groggily and I gave her the thumbnail sketch of what had happened, then handed the phone over to someone to give her directions. She would leave later that morning and come to me straightaway. Arrangements were made for someone to pick her up at the train.

Carefully dressing in a sweater and loose pants, I avoided the dining hall, though I was ravenous. Someone ordered me soup for breakfast and I ate it greedily, sitting up in my bed. My body was depleted from the experience and needed nourishment. As soon as I finished, my fears returned. I began to fear that he would come for me. After all, I'd left him my dorm room number, hoping for a chance to confront him on my turf. How fucking stupid.

And then I got scared for Jim. Where was he? Did he get out? Did they hurt him, too?

In my panic, I began screaming for Jim, thinking they had killed him or kidnapped him, as he was the one who knew me. It took three people to hold me down and tell me he was just fine and had no idea what had happened. He assumed I had gone home, tired of waiting for him. He was at class, they said. Thank God.

Meg arrived late that day. She burst into my room and found me still in a ball under my covers. We embraced and she told me it would all be okay. We cried together. I asked her not to tell her mom, who would tell my parents, and I did not want them to know. I needed to process it on my own. I could do it myself, I thought. Stacey, my resident adviser, was not around that weekend, so Meg said she would stay with me for the weekend and take care of me.

If on Friday my biggest fear had been that the rapist would come to find me, by Saturday night my desire to confront him had become an obsession. My friends and I ordered pizza and sat in the hallway of my dorm. Girls were running in and out of the bathrooms, readying themselves for the night's rush parties. I wished to God those girls wouldn't go out at all.

I got up to go to the bathroom and Meg came with me—she hadn't left my side since her arrival. We were washing our hands in unison, chatting away, when one of the girls came in, harried. Someone was in my room, she said. A friend? I bolted out of the restroom, Meg in tow, to see William Beebe and one of his buddies leaving my room. We locked eyes. Then they sprinted away down the hall, leaving me screaming after him. I noticed his jacket in his hands as he ran. As their footsteps retreated, I almost passed out with fear. How dare he come here without notice? How dare he come here at all? Then, I saw it.

In thick black marker, on my door, was scrawled in huge, loopy handwriting: "It is in your best interest to call me at 804.xxx.

xxxx. If you know what's good for you, you'll call me. Sincerely, William Beebe."

"Meg, get my camera. Get it now. Get a camera, someone get a camera."

A photo wouldn't protect me, but I felt I needed evidence. We took a snapshot of the door and his macabre note. What did he mean by that? Did he hope I would not report him? Had word gotten back to Phi Kappa Psi that I was telling people what had happened? My friends agreed that this was threatening. Now we were all scared. Our fear turned to indignation and anger as we decided, aided by some liquid courage and the egging on of others, to go to Phi Kappa Psi that night and strike back. I don't know what we were thinking. I felt powerless, and we were all frightened, and we went to throw rocks through the glass panes of Phi Kappa Psi's back door. We found the largest rocks we could throw and lobbed them at the house. They crashed through windows, glass shattering everywhere. No one came to stop us, so we kept doing it. No one noticed. I had come to fight back, to make him scared like I was. But even with all these allies, I had only proved myself powerless. Years later, watching the film *Forrest Gump*, I was reminded of that day. There is a scene where the character of Jenny, who had long been molested by her father, visits her childhood home and throws rock after rock, before crumpling to the ground, exhausted. Forrest, the idiot savant, sums it up: "Sometimes, there just aren't enough rocks."

I went home, still feeling vulnerable. In fact, Meg and I slept that night with a dresser shoved against the door and a chair under the handle, terrified that Beebe could come back. We slept fitfully, and when we awoke in the morning, Meg insisted I couldn't live like this. I had to take it a step further and report it properly. My resident adviser, Stacey, was coming home that day from a weekend away. I would start by telling her.

Stacey was a fourth-year English major, who prided herself on her 4.0 GPA. She also took her job as RA very seriously. She was sassy, smart, and ruled with an iron hand. If anyone on the hall was caught drinking, smoking, or causing a disturbance, she'd be at their door in a heartbeat.

When Meg and I knocked on her door and said we had a confidential matter to discuss, Stacey was all business. I told her the whole story, even the incident with the rocks. Stacey acted as though she had heard this story before. She told me to wait in my room, that she had some phone calls to make.

That was it?

We went back to my room. We waited. A while later, Stacey knocked softly. She had phoned Dean Angela Davis to tell her the news. Would I speak with her? Of course. I was beginning to feel like someone was listening to me.

Dean Davis phoned me immediately after Stacey left and agreed to meet with me in the office of the dean of students, Robert Canevari, on Monday afternoon. Finally, someone who could help. Meg and I went about our day with a sense of relief.

The following morning, my bruising and swelling had only become more apparent. My cheekbone had an obvious bruise, my lip was swollen, and the black-and-blue finger marks on my arms became more pronounced. Breathing was still a challenge, as my ribcage felt constricted. On top of that, I was still intermittently bleeding vaginally. My appointment with the deans was that afternoon, but Meg insisted that I couldn't just wait until then. I needed to see someone at Student Health.

We pushed through the front door and I signed the register, handing over my student identification card. The receptionist asked why I was there. The waiting room was crowded with other students. I whispered that I had been raped. Her mouth made a silent O shape and she swiveled on her chair, shuffling some papers. She had me fill out a health history and evaluation, and said someone would be with me soon.

Sure enough, they called my name within minutes, and I was led to an examination room. Meg came with me and held one of my hands as I changed into a gown. I was shivering. The nurse practitioner's name was Marge. She had a red bouffant and a soft Virginia accent. She was kind, but told me Meg would have to leave the room for the examination. She explained what she would be doing, all the while asking questions about that night. Had I showered? Douched? Urinated? Eaten? Brushed my teeth? At this point, of course I had done most of those things. I found myself wishing that I had come here first, instead of the hospital, but I had had no way of knowing that they would send me away. She had me slide down to the bottom of the examination table and put my feet in the stirrups. I had never had a gynecological exam before. I had never had the need, as I was not sexually active. The nurse told me it would be uncomfortable, and told me to breathe deeply. I stared ahead, focusing on my white gym socks. She didn't do a rape kit as we know it today, but I remember her using words like "tears" and "lacerations" as she shined a pen light at my genitals and swabbed the area with a stinging antiseptic. An assistant nurse held my hand. Marge said I had definitely been penetrated.

I stared at the ceiling wondering when it would be over, but knowing this would be crucial evidence if William Beebe was going to be held accountable. A tear rolled down my cheek, and I prayed.

Nurse Marge took my blood pressure and temperature and examined my bruises. I was asked to flex my extremities, bend over and touch my toes, read an eye chart. She asked me if I had reported the incident. I told her I'd been to the emergency room and bailed out. She didn't look surprised. I also said I was going to see the deans that day. "Good," she said. "They'll take care of this."

"I'm so sorry," she said.

"Me, too," I said.

She sent me on my way with contact information for the Peer Sexual Health Educators, a student-run group. "In case you have herpes, you'll need them," she said. Oh my God. She calmly explained that about 20 percent of the university population had herpes at this point—but this brought on a whole new wave of fear. *What if I was pregnant?* Jesus Christ, I hadn't even thought of that. I asked her if I could be pregnant as a result. She said to wait four weeks and if I had not begun menstruating by then, to come back and they would run a pregnancy test. Crash.

Meg and I had a quick, somber lunch on the Corner and she

headed back to the dorm, where Jonathan was waiting to take her to the train station. She needed to get back to school and I needed to let her go. She had been so strong for me, but I needed to stand on my own now. We said our tearful good-byes and I promised to call her to make sure she got home safely and to report back the results of my meeting. I watched her walk in the sun, black hair swinging in the light as she got farther away from me.

Alone, I made my way at the appointed time to see Deans Davis and Canevari at his office. I walked in, shook hands all around, and sat in a chair across from his massive desk. Dean Davis sat off to the side.

Dean Bob Canevari was a handsome, powerfully built man with a mane of salt-and-pepper hair. He dressed conservatively, but in a dapper way. He was an old-school administrator with a great deal of power, and, whether or not true, it was rumored that he still resented the university's being made coeducational. It was well known that he hosted Friday night cocktail parties for male students only. (His own very smart daughter went on to become a professor at the university.)

"So, Dean Davis tells me you've had a problem," Dean Canevari said. "How can I help you?"

I rolled through my whole story again, in full detail. It was exhausting to tell it again.

"Okay, so what you're saying is that this young man forced you to have sex against your will. Did you say no?"

"Of course I did," I said.

I was sitting across from this man with my bruised face and a split lip.

"Was he a boyfriend or a suitor?" he asked.

"No, he was a stranger. I've never met him before in my life. I am, er—I was a virgin."

"Well, you know these parties can get out of control," he said.

"Yes, it was out of control. They fed me a green drink and a stranger dragged me into his room. I was raped. But what do I do now? How can you help me?" Dean Canevari leaned forward. "Are you sure you didn't have sex with this young man and now you regret it? These things happen. It's okay to admit that." He smiled over his desk.

"No!" He wasn't listening to me. "I am telling you I was raped. He had drugs in his top dresser drawer!"

"Drugs?" he asked. "What kind of drugs?" Drugs, apparently, constituted a "real" problem, one worthy of his attention.

"I don't know. I've never done drugs." I said.

"Then how do you know they were drugs?"

"Because I watch television. I'm not stupid."

At this point, Dean Davis had to excuse herself. She had other business to attend to. She placed her hand on mine as she crossed the room to the door. I was left on my own with Canevari.

"Could you tell me where this happened, where the drugs were?"

"Yes, the drugs were in his top dresser drawer, but that's not why I'm here. I was raped, and I know there were lots of people who saw it happen."

"People saw it?" He looked concerned now.

"Yes . . . I was in and out of consciousness, but I know there were other people in the room, watching it happen."

He frowned. This was trouble. He sat quietly for a moment, considering me.

"How do you know his name?" he asked finally. I felt like he was trying to catch me at something, or trip me up.

"I looked through his mail the next morning. He left a threatening message on my dorm door yesterday," I said.

"Well, these are very serious allegations you're leveling. Do you understand that?"

"Yes, sir, I do. I took pictures of the door. What are you going to do?"

I had been attacked, raped, bloodied, bruised. I was dumbfounded at the calm manner in which he was conducting this meeting, seemingly without much concern. I felt the same hopelessness and frustration I had experienced at the ER that first morning. Instinctively, I got up out of the chair to leave.

"No, sit back down. Please, Miss Schimpf, sit back down," he said.

"Call me Liz," I said coolly. I realized I had some power in this situation after all. It was important that I stay and accomplish what I had come here to do. I tried to be direct, to get down to business.

"Has the fraternity been locked down? Are there witnesses being questioned since you got word of this? Have the police been called?" I asked.

He leaned back in his chair, then forward, then steepled his fingers and said to me, "Well, we like to handle these things internally and take care of our own. If it's a university problem, then there's a university solution. And besides, that house is not in Charlottesville police jurisdiction, so we wouldn't call the Charlottesville police, of course."

Oh. Okay. I accepted what he said.

"So, who do we talk to?" I pressed.

"Well, certainly, given the seriousness of your allegations, I'm going to speak to the young man in question," he said.

"Okay, and then what?"

"Have you been seen by a doctor?" he asked.

"The hospital ER wouldn't see me, but I went to Student Health this morning."

"And what did they say?"

"They didn't say anything. They examined me. As you can tell, I've been roughed up."

He squinted. "You do seem to have a bit of a bruise there."

"I took pictures of all of the bruises. I know we'll need some evidence, right?"

"Well, how far do you want to take this?" he asked.

"That's why I'm here. To figure out my options."

"Well, once I have a chance to interview the young man, you'll have a variety of remedies. You can speak with Peer Sexual Health Educators, the university police, the chaplain—anything we can do to help you out. You might even choose to charge him via the Judiciary System."

"Isn't that run by students?" The student-run Judiciary felt a little like just more rock throwing. I wanted this to go to the proper authorities for criminal action.

"Well, there are a lot of options with Judiciary, but many of them are disciplinary and I think you'll find the experience gratifying."

I wasn't so sure.

"Can you write down his name again? And are you absolutely sure he's not your boyfriend? Things didn't just get a little out of hand?"

I could not believe this guy. I chose not to answer. Instead, I asked, "What else should I do? Should we call the university police?"

"Here's the way we like to do it here. First of all, like I said, the Charlottesville police don't have jurisdiction over that house. But we do have our own university police, so we're going to handle it internally. We like to take care of our own," he repeated.

I'll never forget that. We like to take care of our own; we like to handle things internally. What could I say to that? "I'll talk to Beebe, and then you'll want to call Dean Sybil Todd and she can help you report it to the university police," he said, handing me a piece of paper with those phone numbers. At least it was a step up from the student Judiciary process.

Canevari leaned back, very cowboy-like and said, "I'll talk to the young man and we'll see where we go from there." It was clear this meeting was over.

"Wait. Do you need my phone number?" I asked.

"I am sure I can find it, or Dean Davis will have it."

At that moment I realized that he had not taken any notes in our meeting. Not one. I stood up to leave, then paused.

"Dean Canevari? I'd like to tell my parents myself. So, my one request is that they not be notified. They were opposed to me coming to college so far from home in the first place and this will just kill them."

He nodded his head. Then he walked me to the door, shook my hand, and bid me good day.

I walked back home in a daze. I still hoped that Dean Canevari would see the gravity of the situation, that he would help take care of this and have William Beebe arrested.

I called Dean Canevari's office frequently for the next week or so, each time getting a secretary and no return call. Complicating matters, my parents were expected to arrive in Charlottesville in less than two weeks for Parents' Weekend. I didn't know how I would face them. I wanted to tell them, but didn't want to make them worry. And I didn't know how to hide my obvious distress, which only grew with each passing day and unreturned phone call. In those weeks, instead of dressing up for classes, I began to wear jeans and sweaters, even though it was the height of the Virginia fall fashion parade. I cared less about my appearance. Instead of studying outside at the Amphitheatre, a popular gathering spot for those soaking up the last sun of the season and scoping out the opposite sex, I banished myself to the Cave, a smoke-filled bohemian enclave for philosophy students who listened to the Cure.

Dean Canevari finally called me back on the Thursday before Parents' Weekend and asked me to come over to his office to meet with him and Associate Dean of Students Sybil Todd. I hadn't called her—I had been waiting to hear about Dean Canevari's interview with William Beebe. Dean Todd was a warm, round, southern woman, with an accent like Paula Deen and fluffy blonde hair. She wore polished suits and perfect Ferragamo low-heeled pumps. She hugged me warmly at this first meeting, and I latched on to her immediately. Dean Canevari, on the other hand, eyed me with a steely gaze. He had something to tell me.

"I spoke with the young man. He said the sex was consensual. He did not deny that he was intoxicated, but he believed it was what you wanted."

I was devastated. "It was not consensual. He raped me. I don't know how I can be any clearer." I started to cry. "What else can I do? I am not giving up on this. You have to help me."

He gestured to Dean Todd. "If it makes you feel any better, you can go with Dean Todd and she'll take your statement. She can take you to the university police if you so choose." Dean Todd looked at me with sadness.

Statement? Had I not made a statement to Canevari? To Dean Davis? To Student Health? Why had they not interviewed any witnesses? Questioned all the brothers in the fraternity house that night? Of course Beebe would deny it, but why would the investigation stop there? Fine, I thought, I'll make a statement. Another statement.

"Besides," said Canevari, "this kid is no longer a threat to you. He's left the university."

What?

"But I thought he denied it. And we haven't even told the

university police yet. Was he expelled because this violated the Honor Code?"

"No, he didn't violate the Honor Code—that is only for lying, cheating, and stealing. He had been having some academic problems. He left of his own volition."

So, if you cheat on an exam, you can get kicked out of Mr. Jefferson's Academical Village, but if you rape a fellow student you can just quietly slip away? When had he left? And why had no one told me? Were they sure he was never coming back? Canevari seemed unwilling to give me any further information. He bade me good-bye and led Dean Todd and me to the door. We walked over to her office in Garrett Hall. The office seemed like a perfect expression of her—warm and inviting, filled with fresh flowers, photos in silver picture frames, and mementos of her life in Texas. She was gracious, concerned, and maternal. I still couldn't bear the thought of telling my actual mother, but I opened up to Dean Todd immediately. I told her the whole story again, of the rape, the ER, and my meeting with Canevari, not even trying to disguise my contempt for him. She nodded, she listened, and she wrote notes. She asked who was there that night, whom she might be able to speak with. Since I was so new to the university, I still didn't know a lot of faces, but I named Jim, Hudson Millard, Cricket, and a few people I had happened to see there.

"Dean Todd, may I still go to the university police?"

"Why, of course you can, sugar. I'll take you there myself whenever you're ready."

Phew. I felt so much better. And I was ready to go to the university police. But still, I put it off just a little bit longer. I didn't know what would be involved once I set that in motion, and my parents were arriving the next day.

On Friday, as I sat in a late class, my mom and dad were at a cocktail party to welcome first years and their parents. A girl from my dorm introduced herself to my parents, saying how sorry she was for what had happened. My parents asked what she meant. She faltered and stammered, "Um, you better ask Liz. She really needs you right now."

My parents became panicked, frantically calling my dorm room from a pay phone outside. I returned home from class to a ringing phone, but when I answered, it was Dean Canevari. My parents were in his office.

"You better get down here right now and tell them exactly what's going on." My heart about leaped out of my chest. I had told him that I wanted to tell my parents on my own terms. He had let me down once again. I told him I'd be right there.

In Canevari's office, my parents were looking anxious and deeply concerned. I wondered what their biggest fear was at that moment. Maybe that I was being kicked out of school.

"Now, Liz, why don't you tell your parents what's been happening?"

I could not. Could not. Would not.

I turned to face them. "I was at a fraternity party and I saw one of the members doing drugs. He's been threatening me . . ." I trailed off. It was a weak lie.

"You need to tell them what you've told me," Dean Canevari barked at me.

The story he still did not believe.

"Mom, Dad, I was raped at a party by a boy I'd never met. It was awful, but I am fine now and I don't want you to worry. Dean Todd and Dean Canevari are helping me out."

I will never forget the look on my father's face. He began to cry. His only child, his daughter, had been violated under this school's watch and I knew he blamed himself for letting me come here. I was not crying. I knew I had to be strong for them. I kept repeating that I was fine. Once my dad recovered, he had questions.

"Have the police been called?"

"Well, as I explained to Liz," Dean Canevari said, "the fraternity house in question is not under Charlottesville police jurisdiction, but it can be investigated by the university police. We're working on that now. We've spoken to the young man and he denies it, but he has left the university for other reasons." In front of my parents, the dean was no longer in cowboy mode. He was projecting pure, rational authority, trying to assure them that he was on the case and in control.

My mom, silent until this point, turned to me with sadness in her eyes.

"What were you wearing?" she asked me quietly.

"What do you mean?"

"What did you have on when it happened?"

I lost my calm. "Mom, I was wearing a sweater and a skirt. What does that have to do with it?" I was screaming.

My father shut her down. My mother was merely a product of her generation, one in which this question was expected.

Of course, my mother would support me fully in the weeks

and years to come, but in her Irish Catholic world, polite people did not discuss such things. Her very understandable coping mechanism was to bury it away and act like nothing had happened. I respect that it helped her get through it, but it left me feeling disconnected and isolated during that time.

After my outburst, Canevari seemed uncomfortable. He tried to connect man-to-man with my dad, saying things like "Boys will be boys" and "We see a lot of this sort of thing. It's called 'date rape' and there's not much we can do about it." My dad just looked at him, slack-jawed, having none of it.

Finally, Canevari took another approach. "Look, I think Liz should take the semester off, get her act together. Or, if she'd like to transfer, I can make that happen very quickly. Perhaps she'd be happier at Clemson, Duke, or another good school . . . I have contacts."

My dad looked at me. "Honey, do you want to start over? It's okay if you do. The dean here can take care of this and you can go somewhere else. I don't think you should stay here. It's not safe."

Canevari interjected, "Oh, no, it's a very safe school. That's not what I'm saying. I am thinking that Liz is troubled and maybe a change of scenery, whether home or another school, might do *her* some good."

I glared at all three of them. No way. I was staying put. I had earned this.

"I didn't do anything wrong. I don't understand why I should be punished for the actions of another person, a criminal. I'm staying here."

"Well, that's up to you, Liz," said Canevari. "But if you change your mind, your parents will have my phone number and my support."

At that point, I got up and left. I told my parents I'd see them at dinner, that I had some work to do. I needed to get out of that stuffy room and shake off the conversation.

My dad went to speak with a university chaplain, seeking his counsel. A deeply religious man, my dad believed in the goodness of people, and thought this man of the cloth might care enough to spur someone into action. Ultimately, though, that chaplain was just another part of the closed university system.

Mom, Dad, and I went about Parents' Weekend activities, not really speaking of what had happened. They would ask how I was feeling and I would say, "Fine." I tried to let them see the normal parts of my collegiate life, introducing them to the friends I had made, showing them my classrooms and the places I hung out. Still, when it came time to leave, Dad made me promise that I would call him every night at ten P.M. If I ever didn't feel safe, he said, or if something felt wrong, he'd fly down right away and collect me.

I had never been so relieved to see two people leave. Their grief must have been bottomless, but I needed to move forward. My first step would be to finally take my story to the university police.

With Sybil Todd at my side, I went many times to the university police, a privatized police and security group, employed to deal with campus crimes—mostly break-ins, theft of personal property, and any sort of student protest. They were housed in an ugly salmon-colored building far from campus. Dean Todd and I went and I told my story once again. But, once again, I noticed that no notes were taken. The officers sat respectfully and listened to me, but they weren't hearing me.

A couple of months later, we returned to the station for a follow-up meeting, to see if any of the witnesses whose names Dean Todd provided had been questioned, or if the officers had done anything with the statement I had made in our previous meeting. I wanted resolution. Dean Todd conducted her own interviews with the people at the party whom I knew. The university police completed an "investigation," but there were no reliable witnesses. No one at the fraternity was speaking, and Beebe was gone. At Dean Todd's suggestion, I spoke out in another way—the student press. I gave anonymous interviews to the student newspapers, and they wrote about my rape as one of many. The fight against campus rape was very much a grassroots movement at this point. I wanted everyone to be put on notice. Most of all, I didn't want other college girls to suffer similar fates.

Still, although other students wanted to hear what I had to say, I realized the university authorities had effectively silenced me. My case was cold. Sybil Todd and I continued to meet each week for lunch or coffee, but she was really only there for moral support. She was my appointed "maternal figure," since Canevari didn't want to deal with a "female issue."

I would call the university police every once in a while, but I was always told there was no new information. Finally, they stopped returning my calls and I, too, stopped calling them. By end-of-term exams in December, I focused my attention on my coursework and forged forward with the rest of my life.

It was over. They had won.

One day, perhaps a year later, I found the outfit I had worn on the night of the rape at the bottom of a closet in a new house I was renting off-campus with Caroline and several other girls. I had forgotten about these clothes and I wept as I opened the bag. This would never be evidence. I told my housemates that I was going to study and jammed the bag of clothes in my backpack. At the Lucky Seven convenience store on the Corner, I bought some lighter fluid. It was dark and cold as I walked across the Grounds to a cemetery on the fringes. I found a trash can and placed the bag in it. Dousing everything with fluid, I lit a match and dropped it. My clothes ignited in a ball of billowy flames as I sat on the cold red dirt and cried.

CHAPTER 5 *The Legacy of Rape*

I had been determined not to let the rape destroy the rest of my college years, and the remainder of my time at Virginia was pretty typical. I made lots of friends, partied, dated a little bit. I went to football games and movies and fell in love with Latin American literature. I even joined a sorority, Alpha Phi. I didn't want the horror of that night at Phi Kappa Psi to preclude for me the close friendships and community that had made Greek life on campus appeal to me in the first place, and many of my sorority sisters became lifelong friends. For a time I steered clear of the Phi Kappa Psi house—or as far as I could, considering it was just a few doors down from my own sorority. Even with William Beebe gone, I was scared and ashamed to be recognized by someone who had seen my assault. But eventually I felt as indistinguishable as the next coed. Keeping in touch with Dean Todd, I still made small attempts to change the landscape of sexual assault on campus, through anonymous interviews and forums. But the rape was definitely not the focus of my college experience.

I saw William Beebe only once more, under circumstances so surreal it was hard for me to believe afterward what had happened. It was a spring evening in my third year, and I was hanging out with my sisters at the sorority house. We had ordered pizza to be delivered and I had collected the money. When the doorbell rang, I was the one who ran to the door.

Crash.

There, in a delivery uniform, stood Beebe. He was unmistakable. And he knew me. He recognized me. He looked as frightened as I was. Many times I had imagined confronting him, shaking him until he admitted what he had denied to the dean, forcing him to cower with shame for the irreparable harm he had done. But now I just fumbled with the wad of bills in my hands, shoving them at him without waiting to hear the total or calculate the tip. I grabbed the pizza boxes from his hands, slammed the door, and double-locked it. I stood at the window, watching him climb down the stone steps from our house and into the delivery vehicle, while I tried to breathe.

I dropped the pizza boxes and shoved them across the floor, into the chapter room. My heart was pounding as I crawled up the stairs to my room and collapsed on the bed. I had been trying to act normal, to feel normal, but seeing Beebe again tore me apart. I felt like I was experiencing the trauma all over again. The truth was, the scars would last long after college.

Two months before graduation, I fell in love with a law student named Dan. He was older, charismatic, good-looking, smart, and funny. What he failed to tell me was that he already had a girlfriend. Actually, she was his fiancée. I didn't know about her until he dumped her to be with me.

After graduating, I accepted an entry-level position at Grey

Advertising in New York and moved back into my parents' house. But every Friday, I would board the Amtrak train in Penn Station to visit Dan in Baltimore, where he was studying for the bar exam. Our relationship flourished and soon I quit my job and moved to Baltimore to be with him. We were back in New York for my twenty-third birthday when he proposed to me under the Christmas tree at Rockefeller Center with a beautiful diamond ring. We married in a gorgeous ceremony at my childhood church and honeymooned in Aruba. We bought a beautiful townhouse in the historic Bolton Hill section of Baltimore. I set up house and spent my days decorating and my evenings entertaining his colleagues. It seemed like a fairy tale, but it was quite the opposite. My smart and successful new husband turned out to be a womanizing cad with a volatile personality and anger-management problems. Many of my friends did not enjoy his company, and soon I noticed that the other law firm wives we socialized with did not like him.

Even during the times I thought I was happy, I would occasionally suffer what my husband and I called "the wave." We would be out at a restaurant or walking on the beach, and I would feel suddenly ill. Nausea and terror would sweep over me. It usually lasted only a few minutes, but it would leave me sweating and exhausted on a bench or sidewalk, struggling to catch my breath.

When my husband's volatile temper escalated to the point where I could no longer stay, I packed a few suitcases one night and left. Our divorce was obviously acrimonious. He came from a family of lawyers and they all helped represent him. I had no money—Dan had encouraged me to be a stay-at-home wife for the most part, and I had signed a prenuptial agreement three weeks prior to our wedding. His family actually hired an attorney to represent me in the divorce.

I started working at a local catering and event-planning firm and found the work very satisfying. I also found a place to stay—a co-worker was just moving in with her boyfriend and needed someone to care for her own house in the suburbs of Baltimore. Eventually I began dating again—Tom, a young chef I worked with. He was everything my ex-husband was not: mellow, unassuming, and unconcerned with class or monetary status. Since we worked together, we kept our relationship quiet at first, but finally moved in together after a year of dating.

It was soon after my divorce was made final, on the morning of my twenty-ninth birthday, and I was getting ready for work. Tom had had a small birthday party for me the night before and had let me sleep in a bit. I brewed some fresh coffee, watched the morning news, ran the dishwasher, and made a grocery list for later. Our new puppy, a birthday gift, was scratching at his crate to be let out. Suddenly, I could not breathe. My limbs turned purple and blue with cold, my head was red and hot, and my heart was pounding so hard I could see it move in my chest. Death felt certain, the terror was so great. My coffee mug dropped to the floor and I crawled on my hands and knees to the phone in the kitchen. It was a wall-mounted phone, so I had to shimmy up the wall and knock down the cord to grab the handset. It was all I could do to punch the numbers 9-1-1.

"This is the operator, what is your emergency?"

"Help. Heart attack. Send someone. Now," I gasped into the phone. I could still hear my puppy scratching.

"What is your address, ma'am?" asked the female voice.

"I don't . . . I can't . . . Please. Just come."

I began to scream. Sirens wailed and I remember seeing two paramedics over me, working on me. They strapped a blood pressure cuff on me and stuck heart monitors all over me. "Please don't let me die. It's my birthday today," I wailed.

"Honey, you ain't gonna die today, not on my watch," said a kindly EMS worker as he helped me up and led me to the back of the truck. I believed him, but I wanted to know what was wrong with me.

They loaded me onto a stretcher and the waves of panic waxed and waned. Once at the hospital, I don't recall much except a profusion of doctors and nurses hooking me up to intravenous fluids, and a loud beeping noise that was a heart monitor. On some level, I was convinced I was already dead. I thought of my family, of Tom, of the children I would never have.

Then Tom was there, coming through the curtain. He looked concerned but calm. A young doctor came in behind him and asked questions about what was going on in my life. I admitted that I had been in the middle of a terrible divorce, but that I did not feel as though that was enough to provoke a heart attack. I worked out; I was healthy. But I was also adopted and did not know my family history.

"Heart attack? You haven't had a heart attack. You are the healthiest specimen I have seen today," he said. He said that all of the tests had come back negative—EKG, blood count, respiration, etc., and that perhaps I was simply stressed, tired, or hungry. Perhaps I had had an adverse reaction to caffeine, an allergy attack. He gave me a bottle of pills and told me to follow up with my internist. I was dumbfounded. I had felt certain I was going to die, yet there was no clear diagnosis.

Over the next few days, certain that something more serious was wrong with me, I followed up with my internist and two cardiologists, but they all gave me a clean bill of health. I saw a therapist, too. But mostly, I stayed home, scared that the mystery illness would strike again. I still made it to the office and back, but there were no movies, no dinners out, no trips to the store. I became a hermit.

New Year's Eve, there was a terrible ice storm and black ice coated the roads and the trees. Tom and I stayed in and made a special dinner of lobster, foie gras, and champagne. We were toasting the promise of a new year when I felt the symptoms begin again. My hands were cold and purple and my heart had begun to palpitate. Though the roads were icy and treacherous, Tom drove me straight to the hospital. By the time I got there, my symptoms were easing up and again it was impossible to determine what might be wrong. I was incredibly frustrated.

In the next few weeks, still suffering intermittent, milder attacks, I started seeing my therapist more frequently. I stayed home from work. One afternoon I switched on the television. *The Oprah Winfrey Show* was on, and the focus of the program that day was panic disorders. A woman about my age was tearfully describing her symptoms and medical journey. She had the rapid heartbeat, the fear, the feeling of going crazy, the lack of medical explanation, and the battery of tests, and had morphed into an agoraphobic, someone who never leaves the house. My jaw dropped—it mirrored my story exactly. An expert came on and spoke of these "panic attacks" as part of an anxiety disorder closely related to or coexistent with post-traumatic stress disorder. It was, he said, the body's way of dealing with distress or trauma that was locked away. It could strike anyone, but mostly it struck people who had been victims of domestic, sexual, or child abuse, those who had witnessed violence, war veterans, victims of crime where bodily harm took place, and so forth. He went on to explain that the first attack usually struck in a patient's twenties or thirties and that the average sufferer saw sixteen different health professionals before getting the proper diagnosis and treatment. I literally ran to call my therapist. Her secretary told me I could come first thing in the morning. The next morning I felt better than I had in weeks, as I burst into my therapist's office.

I told her about the *Oprah* show, and what I had learned about panic disorder, and she said that she had begun to suspect that might be what I had. She didn't stop me or tell me to slow down. She said that the long-buried trauma of my rape, combined with my abusive marriage and divorce proceedings, probably triggered the attacks. She ordered me off caffeine and all stimulants, told me to practice deep breathing and meditation, and gave me a prescription to treat my anxiety and the acute attacks.

Gradually, my life renewed itself. I still had attacks every so often, but with the medication, I felt in control. Tom and I took a vacation in Mexico, and I returned to work feeling much better.

And then things changed all over again.

A few months later, Tom accepted a career-changing transfer to Philadelphia to be an apprentice to Chef Michel Richard, of Citron and Citronelle fame. I decided it was time for me to move on as well. Serendipitously, a former colleague and dear friend called me about a job opening as a sales manager at the historic Hay-Adams Hotel in Washington, D.C. I jumped at the chance to work with old friends and to change my landscape. I still visited Tom in Philadelphia when I could, but increasingly he felt just like a supportive best friend. I moved in with a friend on Capitol Hill and I settled into a new routine, determined to make a fresh start in a new city. Friends old and new helped bring me out of my fearful shell. I began to go out again—to the store, the gym. I was no longer agoraphobic. I was making progress and was so grateful to have the beginning of a genuine life again.

In June of 1996, after a business trip to New York, I disembarked from the Amtrak train at Union Station in Washington. I called my roommate to ask for a ride home, but he explained he was hosting a dinner party. Could I take a cab home? Not really wanting to go home to a party in full swing after a long business trip, I opted to wait it out and grab a bite to eat at the round restaurant and bar in the center of the station. I ordered a sandwich and a glass of wine, then took out my planner and jotted notes from my sales calls in New York. Looking up from my notes, I noticed a young, strikingly handsome man sitting about six seats away at the bar. He was looking through a hefty document and had his tie tucked into his dress shirt as he attempted to eat a rather large sandwich. We locked eyes, and his kind look and smile hit me like a wall. I felt like I had come home. To this day, I cannot explain it.

Walking over to me, the man introduced himself as Mike Seccuro. He explained that he was waiting to take a train home to Baltimore, after spending the day in long meetings. He worked as an investment banker and traveled to Washington a great deal. He had a wonderful way about him, a quick smile and deep brown eyes that hinted at his clever but sensitive nature. He was quick-witted, hilarious, and insightful. We exchanged business cards and promised, after chatting briefly, to get together. I didn't let myself get my hopes up, though.

Two days later there was a voice mail on my work phone. Mike was coming back to Washington the following week for three days, and would I like to have dinner? He was scheduled to stay at the Hay-Adams, so I had him upgraded to a suite and sent him some fresh fruit and bottled water. To this day he insists that it was purely coincidental that he was booked into the hotel where I worked.

We met on a Monday evening for dinner back at Union Station and fell in love on the spot. As we talked about our pasts, he mentioned that he had gone to the University of Virginia. Fear struck at my heart. Please, God, please let him not know about me. Please let him not be a Phi Kappa Psi. But no, he was a Chi Phi, and he had graduated in 1995, seven years behind me. I hadn't realized he was so young. After that first night, we became inseparable, traveling weeknights to see each other and spending together every moment we could spare from work, going to the zoo, the movies, dinners, and the opera. I loved him in a way I had never loved anyone in my life.

About one month into our relationship, I knew that I had to tell him my story. If I believed in this relationship, I needed to be fully honest about my past and tell him what had happened at our alma mater. On a quiet date, fingers intertwined, I told him everything. He listened intently, and then reached over to hug me. I was sobbing, and scared he might reject me, thinking I was "damaged." Instead, he told me he loved me. I had indeed come home.

Through ups and downs, panic attacks, relocations, and separations, our love grew stronger. On November 13, 1999, we married in a church in Atlanta, Georgia. I had found my partner, my rock.

When Mike got a job on Wall Street, we moved to New York, and I found work as an event planner. On Christmas Day, 2002, we welcomed our first child, Ava Noelle. Holding her that day, I realized how far we had come. How far I had come. We moved to Greenwich when Ava was one year old and I began my own event-planning company, which flourished. Life was a miracle, and when I looked at my family with such joy and pride, the nightmares of the past seemed very far behind me.

And then, that September day in 2005, the letter arrived. And the nightmare was back.

CHAPTER 6

The Charges, the Arrest, and the System

On January 5, 2006, Police Chief Timothy Longo of Charlottesville stood on the steps of City Hall in front of a smattering of reporters and other local media and read the following statement:

> In mid December 2005, a thirty-eight-year-old Connecticut woman came forward to report a sexual assault that had occurred some twenty-one years ago.
>
> According to the victim, the incident occurred in October 1984 while visiting the Phi Kappa Psi fraternity house, located in the one hundred block of Madison Lane in Charlottesville, Virginia. Both she and her assailant were students at the University of Virginia at the time. This was not a "date rape." The assailant was a stranger to the victim at the time of the assault.
>
> In the months prior to reporting this incident, the victim reports having been contacted by her assailant. She has not seen or otherwise had contact with this person since approximately two years after her attack, sometime in 1986.
>
> During the course of these most recent contacts by her

assailant, the victim was able to discern the subject's where-abouts. It was shortly thereafter that she reached out to us in hopes of bringing this person to justice.

Detectives have met with the victim, conducted an extensive interview with her, and conducted a timely and thorough investigation. Subsequent follow-up investigation of her report was offered to the Charlottesville City Commonwealth's Attorney and based on that a warrant was sought for the suspect's arrest.

On the evening of January 4, 2006, Las Vegas Metropolitan Police arrested Mr. William N. Beebe of Las Vegas, Nevada, pursuant to a Virginia warrant charging him with rape in violation of Virginia State Code 18.2-61. A determination of his extradition status has not yet been determined.

The matter of his return to Virginia to answer the charge is currently being resolved by the Charlottesville Commonwealth's Attorney's office and the authorities in Nevada. UVA is now looking into what was done back then. It was not reported to city police.

UVA spokesperson Carol Wood released a statement that UVA had been "cooperating fully" with police, and had found documentation in the Office of Student Affairs verifying my complaint of 1984. However, Wood said, "We don't comment on ongoing criminal investigations."

And so it began, with a press conference ripple that became a wave of controversy.

* * *

How did we arrive at this point a little more than a month after the darkest days of the Thanksgiving holiday? The end of November brought so many emotions to my household. The e-mails from William Beebe continued to haunt me, and I would intermittently e-mail him. The correspondence was never friendly, to my mind, although my questions were sometimes benign. I was still afraid he might come after me, and I believed that if I stayed in close touch with the predator, he couldn't sneak up on his prey.

Christmas loomed and I did the best I could, decorating a huge Norwegian spruce tree with masses of fairy lights, draping garlands over the banisters, and baking cookies. We took our annual holiday photos and I set about addressing Christmas card envelopes. I went to preschool holiday activities and continued my heavy client workload. But at night, in the quiet cold of Connecticut, I would still sit on my porch, looking at the stars and wondering when the next e-mail would come. Already, William Beebe's reemergence was sending waves through my life. In early December, one of my dear friends, Sarah, brought her kids over for a play date with Ava. As the kids ran wild in the sunny playroom, we discussed preschool and holiday preparations. I hadn't yet opened up to many people about what was happening, and I wanted my friend to know. I told her I wanted to show her something and ran upstairs to get the letter.

She read it, turned it over in her hands, and sighed.

"I'm so sorry, Liz," she said.

"It's crazy, right?"

"Yes, yes it is."

But our discussion went no deeper than that. Instead, she looked at her watch, gathered her children, and begged off, saying she had to make holiday cookies for her daughter's class.

I never received another phone call from her. I saw her at parties and the playground and she always greeted me with a pleasant smile, but there was nothing more there. Sarah was the first, but, sadly, not the only, friend to withdraw when I shared this new development. Many had known about what happened in college, but bringing it into the present was somehow different. Perhaps some people feel that tragedy is contagious and to see it happen to a friend is to acknowledge the possibility of its entering one's own life. Regardless, it hurt deeply to lose friends I had considered a part of my support system.

Corresponding with Beebe had me thinking more about the past, and I'd been doing some Internet research on rape statistics at the University of Virginia and other colleges. Just Googling "University of Virginia rape" brought up an astonishing number of stories on blogs and in area newspapers of those who had been victimized at my alma mater and other area colleges and universities. One Web site was called "UVA Victims of Rape," and it was stunning to me that such a Web site even existed. It began with the story of Susan Russell, whose daughter, a University of Virginia rape victim, not only had been denied justice but had almost been run off campus for reporting her attacker. I felt immediate sympathy for this family. There were dozens of other UVA rape stories as well. Many, like mine, and like Susan's daughter's, were cases that the university did not want to hear, or that they deemed were actually "consensual" sex. Many victims did not even bother to report the rapes for fear of retribution by their attackers or the university.

I was then directed to a local Charlottesville weekly, the *Hook*, which had run an explosive cover story, "How UVA Turns Its Back on Rape." I sat mouth agape as I read about the case of Annie Hylton, another female student who was raped at UVA. She had been unable to criminally prosecute her rapist, but had finally prevailed in civil court. It outraged me that so many women had faced the same problems in dealing with the university administration, and that these cases continued to be mishandled. How big was the problem? I e-mailed the journalist who had penned the story, Courteney Stuart, explained my situation with Beebe, and commended her on her reporting. She e-mailed back, saying that she had received many powerful responses to the story, and asking if she could delve into my story further as a follow-up. Why not? Off the record, we began a correspondence. I told further details of my story and shared some of the e-mails between myself and Beebe. I was finding my voice again, a voice lost so many years ago when I burned my clothing in that trash can.

In the years since my rape, I had become marginally involved with sexual assault advocacy groups, working with other victims. But I felt removed from my own experience, and telling my story to these other victims was not about self-examination or reflection; it was more about helping and feeling as though I could do some good. The fact of the matter was that I was a bit detached from my own trauma and not doing the work I should have been doing on myself. Speaking and e-mailing now with

Courteney during this time of the correspondence with Beebe hit much closer to home.

Next, I started e-mailing with Susan Russell, whose account of her daughter's struggle had first made me realize the scope of this issue. Her daughter's story was particularly painful in that the perpetrator was allowed back on campus and went on to rape another coed. Susan's Web site seemed like a safe space to share ideas with someone of a like mind. We corresponded for a bit and I explained to her that I was denied any sort of resolution because Phi Kappa Psi was not under the Charlottesville police jurisdiction and that I had been advised just to seek a university Judiciary proceeding, a move that was pointless once William Beebe had left the university. Susan e-mailed back that what I said was incorrect. The Phi Kappa Psi house on Madison Lane was indeed part of Charlottesville police jurisdiction.

My brain froze. Could that be true?

Had they lied to me? I was stunned. I looked up the number for the Charlottesville Police Department and found the name of the chief of police, Timothy Longo. That seemed like a great place to start. I wanted to confirm Susan's claim that I had been given incorrect information, but also, now that I was telling my story again, and now that there were new developments, I thought it might be worthwhile finally to tell the actual authorities under whose jurisdiction, as it now seemed, this crime had been committed. From my correspondence, William Beebe seemed erratic, perhaps antisocial. I still feared he might come to try to apologize personally. I wanted to let them know that this person had been e-mailing me and knew my home address.

On December 3, 2005, I picked up the phone, hesitated, then punched in the number to the Charlottesville Police Department. I asked for Chief Longo and was transferred to his personal voice mail box.

"Hi, you don't know me, but I was a student at the university and I was raped by a fellow classmate in 1984 at the Phi Kappa Psi house on Madison Lane and I reported it to all of the deans and the university police. Nothing was done. Through the alumni association, this person has made contact with me again and he knows where I live and I . . . well, I don't know what to do and I just need . . . Sir, I think I need your help. He's been e-mailing me to apologize for the rape and he knows where I live and I am a little concerned. Um, I was told that the Charlottesville police had no jurisdiction over that house, but now I'm not sure and I'm afraid . . . and well, my name is Liz Seccuro, S-e-c-c-u-r-o, and ah, I live in Greenwich, Connecticut." I left my number, thinking he would never call me back. He would probably think I was insane. But forty-five minutes later, my office phone rang.

"Is this Liz Seccuro?" Chief Longo asked.

"Yes! Thank you for calling me back!"

"Can you tell me about what's been going on?"

I gave him a synopsis of what had happened in 1984, what reporting procedures I had been through, the arrival of the letter in September, and what had transpired. He asked if he could see the e-mail correspondence and I agreed readily. He asked if I had notified the Greenwich Police Department, which I had not, and he volunteered to inform them of the situation. He asked questions about the attack itself and how it had been handled. He was charming, polite, strong, and businesslike. I had no idea what was happening, but I kept answering his questions. When I asked, he confirmed that the house on Madison Lane was indeed under CPD jurisdiction and always had been.

"Ma'am, did you realize that there is no statute of limitations on rape in the Commonwealth of Virginia? This person can still be charged with the crime at any time."

Longo and I exchanged e-mail addresses and he gave me the number of his direct line. I felt safe speaking with him, and I agreed to forward him the e-mail correspondence with Beebe as soon as we hung up. Chief Longo told me that either he or one of his detectives would follow up.

I gathered all of Beebe's e-mails to me and mine to him and sent them to Chief Longo, along with some of my notes and a narrative regarding the rape itself, including each detail I could recall. Since I had been corresponding with Susan Russell and Courteney Stuart, it did not take long to gather the information that I felt was necessary.

When Mike returned home late that night, I told him about everything—my research, my conversation with the police chief, and what I had sent over. He listened and assured me that it was smart to contact someone and that maybe now I could rest a little easier. He was right. That night I slept for more than five hours for the first time in a long while.

The sun came up as I made coffee and fed Ava breakfast. My day was filled with busywork and e-mails, planning for Christmas dinner and ordering holiday gifts online.

I had just put Ava down for a nap when there was a sharp knock at the door.

Still in velour sweatpants and a messy ponytail, I looked out to see two police officers standing on my porch.

They showed me their Greenwich Police Department badges when I opened the door.

"Good morning, ma'am," one said. "We have word about your situation from Chief Longo of Charlottesville. He wanted us to come by and get a feel for the house and what's been happening."

"Sure," I said, "come on in." I offered them coffee and they accepted.

One took out a notepad.

They asked to see the letter and some of the e-mails. They asked me questions about my daily routine. They took a good look around and studied the front and back doors, as well as the side windows and the basement access. They asked if I had a security system. I did not.

My house was the only house at the top of a hill, accessible by one road. If a car was coming up the drive, the driver was either lost or destined for my house. The two officers promised to station a patrol car at the bottom of the hill until they received further notice from the Charlottesville Police Department, and I felt more secure when they left.

That evening, after I had put Ava to bed in her crib, the phone rang again. It was Detective Nicholas Rudman of the Charlottesville police. He said he had had a meeting with the chief, had studied all the materials I had sent, and had some questions for me. Would now be a good time?

Detective Rudman walked me through the basics again, asked more detailed questions about the e-mail correspondence and confirmed that the Greenwich officers had made contact.

"Ms. Seccuro, would you be willing to come to Charlottesville and give us a statement?" I pondered the logistics of this and thought, why not? We could make a weekend of it. The last time I had visited Charlottesville was for my fifteenth college reunion, when Ava was six months old. I told him I would do it.

"Great. Ideally, we would like to interview you sooner rather than later."

I didn't quite comprehend the urgency after all this time, but asked if I could call him back.

"Absolutely," he said. "Why don't you make arrangements and let us know when you'll be in town? And, hey, thanks for sharing this with us. What you are doing is very brave. I'm going to be working with my partner, Detective Scott Godfrey, on this, so if you get a call from him, know that it's my partner. I look forward to meeting you."

I phoned Mike at the office and we agreed to go that Friday night and stay for two nights. I called the Boar's Head Inn and booked a room with a crib for Ava. I called Detective Rudman and he said that he and Detective Godfrey would pick me up at the hotel Saturday at noon. I also e-mailed Courteney Stuart at the *Hook* to tell her about these developments, and that I would be coming to town. We agreed to meet while I was there.

On December 9 we checked into our hotel room at the inn. At noon the next day, Detectives Rudman and Godfrey were in the lobby to meet me.

We shook hands all around and they asked if we could take a drive before going down to the station. I sat in the passenger seat of the squad car as we set off down the road toward the main campus, with Detective Rudman behind the wheel and Detective Godfrey in the backseat. We exchanged pleasantries about my drive down, the upcoming holidays, my daughter. I tried to breathe deeply. It was a glorious late-fall day with deep blue skies and brilliant sunshine, the kind of day that always reminded me why I loved Virginia.

"Liz, we wanted to get a sense of your memory. Could you take us to some of the places you mentioned in your statements to us and Chief Longo?" asked Godfrey.

"Sure," I said. As we drove, I pointed out the salmon-colored building that housed the university police and told them of my visits there. I told them a bit about my meetings there with Sybil Todd and the university police. We continued on, stopping near Rugby Road and the Rotunda. I pointed left to the Phi Kappa Psi house, sitting gracefully at the head of Madison Bowl.

"Drive down the street," I urged. We drove past Phi Psi.

I pointed to a few windows. "That's the room I was raped in," I said, gesturing toward the second-floor window on the far right. "If you go around to the other street, there's another window overlooking Madison Lane, and the bed was flush against that window."

"Can you take us the way that you walked to the emergency room?"

"Absolutely. Turn back onto Emmett Street. I walked this way." The emergency room had been renovated, but I showed them where the entrance had formerly been in the rear, where I walked. The memories were hard and I swallowed my saliva.

Next, we doubled back and drove toward the main part of the campus, to my dorm, and parked. We walked in, turned right, and walked up the stairs to the second floor. We turned right, then quickly left, and at the end of the long hall I saw the door to my room.

I touched the door, almost caressing it. I felt overwhelmingly sad as I stood there, feeling so much older, but still so frightened. Rudman knocked and tried to open it, but it was locked. I explained how Beebe had written the threatening note on the door in black marker. They thought perhaps current scientific testing could reveal the words that had been written even after all these years. I showed them the communal bathroom where I had showered, the hallway where I saw Beebe running with his friend after leaving the note and taking his jacket. I pointed out the names of friends who lived in each room and was amazed at my own power of recall. They took copious notes, jotting down every name and room number. They asked me if I could find these people on the alumni Web site and I said that I could.

Continuing our drive around campus, I pointed out the buildings that housed Dean Canevari's office, Dean Todd's office, the various libraries, dining halls, and bookstores. We drove to Chancellor Lane to see my sorority house, where Beebe had delivered the pizzas. The flood of memories was bittersweet, as this was a place I had loved.

Finally, we began our drive to the downtown Mall and the police department, a nondescript building at the very end. We walked into a large conference room, furnished with a large wooden table and a few file cabinets. I sat in a chair as they brought in soft drinks, notepads, and audio equipment. They asked if I was comfortable and if I was ready to tell what had happened to me that night in October 1984.

It had been twenty years since I had spoken about this night in such detail, from beginning to end. Telling it now, especially being back in Charlottesville, was the oddest sensation.

I asked for a piece of paper as I drew a layout of Phi Kappa Psi—the common rooms, the foosball table, the kitchen, the staircase, the second-floor room, the bar. I drew a rough diagram of the room in which I had been raped, mapping out the doorway, the bed, the loft, the sofa, the windows, the closet, the dresser. I drew myself as a stick figure on the bed and on the sofa where I had awoken.

In order to describe Beebe and some of the other brothers, I stood up and asked Detective Godfrey to stand in order to describe height and weight. I took off my high-heeled boots to demonstrate my own height. I could hear the clock on the wall ticking softly.

As we got to the minutes before the attack, I stood to pantomime the chair where Beebe held me down around my waist, the doorway where I was lifted by another brother into Beebe's arms, and the padlocked door where I screamed and pounded for my friend Hud.

And then we came to the part where I had to describe the rape itself. I stumbled frequently, but their questions were calm and direct.

"Where was he touching you?"

"Did he penetrate you with his hands?"

"Did he penetrate you in other ways?"

"Yes," I paused. Did I have to say it?

As if reading my mind, Rudman said, "Liz, I know this is difficult, but you have to tell us where he penetrated you."

"He forced his penis and his hands into my vagina." I started to cry. "I tried to fight him off, but he was so heavy and he was hurting me."

I looked up and saw a tear rolling down Detective Godfrey's face.

"Did you report this to anyone?"

They knew the answers, but they had to go on the record. I described my visit to the hospital, my talks with my resident adviser, and subsequent meetings at the dean's office and with the university police.

My whole statement took over two hours. The story I had kept buried came pouring forth, the details fresh. People were listening to me, hearing me, and I would never be silent again.

"I think we have enough here," said Rudman, clicking off the tape.

I got up to stretch and put my boots back on. Godfrey asked, "Do you have the letter with you?"

Digging in my purse, I offered the letter. He asked to keep it, and made me a photocopy before tucking the original into a file folder. Then, they asked me to sit down again.

Leaning forward, Detective Rudman asked, "Would you like to press charges against William Nottingham Beebe for your rape in October of 1984?"

With that question, a new journey would begin for me. The emotions were too much to bear and I began to sob.

"Yes," I said. "Yes, I would like to press charges, please."

They thanked me for my time, my story, my bravery. They said they'd be in touch with me to explain the next steps, and warned me that the road ahead would be a long one. They gave me their cards and I hugged them both as we exited the conference room.

It had been a long, exhausting day. Mike and Ava were waiting for me when we stepped out into the sunlight.

Rudman and Godfrey introduced themselves and marveled over Ava. I scooped up my daughter and hugged her tightly as we went on our way. I was a normal wife and mother again. Mike attempted to ask me some questions about how it had gone, but I wasn't ready. I wanted my baby girl to see me smiling, so Mike just held my hand and we took Ava to the ice cream shop down the street.

Later that day, I met with Courteney Stuart and her photographer from the *Hook*, Jen Fariello, to continue our interview and have photos taken for the story we were working on. They were both so professional and friendly, putting me immediately at ease, despite the day I had already had. It felt good to unload my story.

The next steps came as soon as we returned to Greenwich. First, the police had to ensure that the e-mail address and computer that the e-mails were coming from indeed belonged to

William Beebe. The computer crimes desk of the CPD contacted me, and we were able to determine conclusively that the e-mails had come from him.

In the following days, I combed through the online alumni directory, providing Rudman and Godfrey with every detail of every witness I could remember. This became a full-time job, but it was good to feel that I was actually doing something for myself, and was no longer stuck staring at my computer screen, anxiously, fearfully awaiting Beebe's e-mails. On December 19, 2005, Rudman and Godfrey flew to Las Vegas to obtain a search warrant for Beebe's home there; they worked with the Las Vegas police. However, two days later, when they set out with Vegas police detectives to visit Beebe's house, there was no one home. When they reached Beebe on his cell phone, he said he was in Florida on a business trip. Rudman questioned him further on the phone, and Beebe admitted that he had indeed written those e-mails to me and that the content was his own writing. He also admitted that he had had sex with me in October 1984 and that I had been incapacitated at the time. Although he wouldn't use the word himself, that, by definition, is rape. Using Beebe's instructions to disarm his home alarm, the police entered the house. They needed evidence in order to obtain an arrest warrant. They seized Beebe's computer, a journal with handwriting that matched that in the letter to me, and an electric bill with his name and address on it, proving residence. On December 23 Godfrey and Rudman traveled back to Charlottesville with the evidence, before joining their families for the holidays.

A few days after Christmas, the police contacted Assistant Commonwealth Attorney Claude Worrell. His job was to ascertain whether there was enough evidence for an arrest and, subsequently, a prosecutable case. Worrell was professional and friendly and I put my faith in him entirely.

But as the days dragged on and no arrest was made, I became very anxious. Unfamiliar with the criminal process, I had no idea how long these things could take. We had a confession, corroboration, evidence—what else did they need? And as I learned more about William Beebe, I became more disturbed. Although he had sent me a business card from his realty office, he had not actually worked as a real estate agent in almost three years. Rather, he was working as a massage therapist, touching the bodies of clients who presumably trusted him. It was becoming increasingly difficult to think of this admitted rapist enjoying a free life. Of course, he had been doing so for years, but now that the wheels were in motion, I needed closure.

On January 4, 2006, Sergeant Rick Hudson, a trusted colleague of Chief Longo, called me. William Beebe was in custody at the Clark County Detention Center in Las Vegas. He had gone without much of a fight. For the first time in ages I felt calm, and safe.

At my computer the next day, I logged onto the corrections center system and typed in his name. Checking the local news stations online, I watched Beebe's arrest footage, but couldn't bear to look at the actual mug shot. I had not seen him since the pizza delivery in 1986. I struggled mightily with that photograph—and still do. It's like staring at the face of evil.

Beebe spent six days in the Vegas jail before being extradited to Virginia. A Charlottesville judge set his bond at $40,000. I felt renewed frustration when Beebe quickly paid the amount and was free again, pending trial.

Beebe hired two well-known Charlottesville criminal defense attorneys, Rhonda Quagliana and Francis McQ. Lawrence, of the firm St. John, Bowling, Lawrence & Quagliana. Ms. Quagliana was a beautiful and accomplished woman, a graduate of the University of Virginia School of Law who was married to a local judge. Men accused of rape often choose female defense attorneys, who might make them seem more sympathetic to juries. Quagliana was a good choice for Beebe and she answered the charges with all guns blazing.

"It was a too-much-to-drink college sex event," Quagliana told the *Hook*, "and it was something that had plagued his conscience for a long time." She said that when Beebe admitted the rape in his e-mails and to police, he was simply following the advice of another victim "who was trying to help him understand where Miss Seccuro was coming from and what her thinking was." In her account, Beebe was shocked when I filed charges, because he had only been "trying to do the right thing . . . Unfortunately, young people in college do things they regret," she said. "He was trying to apologize for one of those things."

Quagliana promised that details would emerge to exonerate her client. "This was bad behavior, poor judgment, immature, and all those other things," she said, "but it was not a rape."

Interest in this case, and controversy surrounding it, was just heating up. A tsunami was headed toward Greenwich. It was called the media.

CHAPTER 7 *The Media Beast and What She Eats*

Commonwealth of Virginia v. William Beebe was the name of the case—the Commonwealth was bringing charges against someone who had broken its laws. I had been just seventeen at the time of the rape, so it was a case of sexual assault against a minor, and as such, I was referred to only as Jane Doe in the filings. Still, my anonymity did not last long. I hadn't anticipated how much interest the media would have in my case, or how quickly they would find me. It didn't help that someone at the Charlottesville juvenile courthouse had neglected to black out my real name in two instances on the indictment. On the day of Beebe's arrest, Chief Longo held his brief, somber press conference on the steps of Charlottesville City Hall. Almost immediately, our home phone—which had always been an unlisted number—and even my cell phone started ringing off the hook with reporters asking for comments. My BlackBerry was abuzz with further requests. I didn't want to make any public statements, and I definitely did not want to say anything that might jeopardize the case. We didn't know what to say on the phone except "She is not available." But the media do not give up easily. By the next morning, the AP wire had picked up the story, and life as I knew it came to an abrupt end. The phone calls were just the beginning. Two days later, laden with a sleepy two-year-old and an SUV filled with groceries, I turned into my driveway in the early evening. At the bottom of the hill on Lake Avenue, news trucks were idling with their lights off, as if I would be too stupid to notice. I gunned my engine and hightailed it up the hill. Parking alongside the house, instead of in the garage, I left my groceries and sprinted into the house through the rear kitchen entrance with Ava in my arms. I slammed the door, locked it, and lowered all of the miniblinds. As if on cue, there was an aggressive slamming of our knocker out at the front door—it was only a matter of time before they found the back entrance.

Mike came into the kitchen and I could only point my finger toward the front door with fright in my eyes. Ava and I crawled underneath the kitchen table. I pretended it was a game and put my finger to my lips with an exaggerated "Shhhhhh . . ." She giggled and became a happy co-conspirator as we huddled together in our secret spot, pretending to hide from Daddy. I didn't want to face the cameras; more important, I didn't want anyone taking pictures of Ava. My first responsibility was to protect her.

Bang! Bang! Bang!

I finally heard the door open and a bit of a scuffle with Mike's loud voice echoing off the walls. He did not sound happy. Leaning out from under my table, I could spy a little throng of lights, cameras, and people. Mike was explaining that I would not be speaking to them, when I whispered to Ava that I would go "find" Daddy. At the door, Mike looked surprised, but I let loose on the little group.

"How dare you come here to a private citizen's home, thinking we don't know our rights? Turn that camera off! Does it really give you a 'story,' following a rape victim home? With her child in the car? Have some grace and class and get off my property." The bunch backed away with some contrition, but not before trying to get a shot. I slammed the door. Then I calmly walked back into the kitchen where Ava was still hiding, and crawled in with her.

"Hey, Ava! It's your turn to hide. Do you think you and Daddy can hide from me? I'll count to one hundred!" She scampered off in her tiny sweater and jeans, looking for her dad.

Mike knew to keep Ava distracted and allow me some space. I stayed curled up under the table, sobbing, for over an hour. I felt violated, preyed upon. And that was only the first of many such encounters. That sort of violation is the very reason so many rape victims avoid going public. The last thing victims need is to lose their sense of safety in their own homes, after their personal and bodily safety has been so seriously compromised. For me, the strain caused flashbacks, and fresh panic attacks.

At this point Mike decided he needed to take some time off from work, to be with me and to help fend off the constant intrusion of the media. He tried to explain the gravity of the situation to his bosses at Bank of America—after all, it was front-page news. But they said they couldn't spare him, a vice president of investment banking, given his heavy workload. After multiple meetings with various departments at the office, it was agreed that Mike could take a week off to help me acclimate, assuming he worked from home and took all conference calls related to his deals. On day three of his "leave," Mike's cell phone was buzzing nonstop. It was obvious that if he wanted to stay on good terms with Bank of America he needed to get back to the office. The corporate behemoth wasn't much concerned with his or his family's well-being. In the end, when the pressure of the case became too great, Mike took a less demanding job in the private banking sector so that he could spend more time with Ava and me.

As coverage of my case became even more widespread, our strict "no comment" policy became harder to maintain. It certainly wasn't protecting us from the uglier side of the media. The producer of one tabloid television show called after my several refusals to be interviewed, saying, "You might as well be cooperative, because we're running the story either way." I again declined, but she was true to her word. That night, accompanied by photos of me they had somehow dug up, they ran the headline teaser "Did Rough Sex and an AA Apology Land This Man in Prison?" It was disrespectful, diminishing, and sickening.

I had decided before Beebe's arrest that sharing my story could do some good, and I began to believe that again. With good reason, Claude Worrell had cautioned me about the risks of going public, but he understood the need to clear the air and start a constructive dialogue. The media already knew my identity. I would be careful not to say anything too controversial. I simply wanted to expound upon the facts that were already out there and clarify any misinformation or incorrect assumptions. Besides, Worrell had been preparing me for the possibility that we might not get a conviction. With no DNA, no police reports, and no witnesses yet coming forward, it could be very difficult to prove Beebe's guilt beyond a reasonable doubt. I wanted to share my story so that even if Beebe was acquitted, people would understand that he was not "innocent." I wanted to raise awareness of the difficulties of so many rape victims in attaining justice. I wanted to give hope to other survivors. Maybe this was a good opportunity after all. "Remember," Worrell told me, "in a rape case, it is never, ever the alleged rapist on trial, whether in the courtroom or in the media. The victim is on trial. Always."

In March 2006, I agreed to my first on-camera interview, for the Charlottesville NBC affiliate. The interview took place in a hotel room in Washington, D.C. In the room were just me, one sound tech, and the reporter. The gentle, soft-spoken reporter asked me questions about that night, the rape itself, the university's response, the letter, what I thought of the arrest, and the forthcoming case. Honestly, I don't recall one bit of what I said. I was so scared I could barely keep my voice modulated, and as kind as the reporter was, I hated every minute of it. Before we wrapped, the reporter asked me if I would be interested in talking to the folks at *Dateline NBC* and handed me the card of a producer. I accepted the card and said I'd think about it.

Back in Connecticut, I was juggling my duties as a mother, wife, and businesswoman with cooperating with the investigation and trying to stanch the flow of media curiosity. In addition, Mike and I had decided to start a nonprofit philanthropic fund for rape survivors and their families. We had already heard from many supporters, and we wanted to turn some of the attention I was getting toward doing good for other survivors. We called it S.T.A.R.S.—Sisters Together Assisting Rape Survivors.

It gave survivors resources to use in the event of a sexual assault and granted funding to qualified organizations dealing with issues of sexual assault, domestic violence, and incest. We were proud to have it up and running quickly, so that media outlets could start featuring it. S.T.A.R.S. thrives to this day, thanks to the generous donations of so many.

One day, I pulled out the business card of the producer from *Dateline*, John Block. I called, he picked up, and I bonded with him immediately. His voice was calm, his humor easy, and his understanding of the case's gravity quite apparent. He was the first journalist to tell me, "I'm so sorry for what has happened to you." John asked for an "exclusive," which basically means you do not tell your story to a competing show or network. Shows on NBC and MSNBC—specifically *Dateline*, *Today*, and *The Abrams Report*—would have the same piece and cross-market it. I agreed. A few weeks later, a crew came out to our home for the interview. Edie Magnus, then an NBC correspondent, was my interviewer. I adored her. She was warm and funny and a mom herself. It was an almost joyful atmosphere the first day of the shoot—we ordered out for food, Ava got to play with some of the equipment, and I just relaxed and conversed with John and Edie about what we'd be covering. Meanwhile, a large crew of audio and video people was draping the windows, moving furniture around, and setting up chairs.

Edie's questions weren't easy. What did I think of William Beebe? Did I forgive him? Did I give him credit for coming forward? What was the rape like? How was I able to begin a normal sex life afterward? What was life like before the letter arrived?

How would I face it if he were acquitted? It was the first of several interviews.

Ava began to recognize the crew. They interviewed my father, my best friend, people who lived on my dorm hall, Chief Longo. They came along to my office. They tracked down other rape victims from the university, witnesses, friends of William Beebe, and even tried to get an interview with Beebe himself. (As expected, he did not cooperate.) I had just one rule: not one shot of Ava could ever be used. By agreeing to the interviews I had opened up my whole life, but I was a mother first, and had to protect her and her anonymity.

An air date in May 2006 was decided upon. The day before the piece was scheduled to air, they asked if I would have a brief conversation, live, with Katie Couric on the *Today* show. Frankly, Katie scared me. A fellow Virginia alum, she had been a Tri-Delta and a Lawn resident—an honor bestowed on only fifty-four UVA students a year, who are chosen to live in the university's original dorm rooms—and I knew she was a big proponent of her alma mater. Still, after some hesitation, I agreed, and the next morning, I found myself in the *Today* show green room, awaiting my segment. John and Edie came down to watch the interview, and seeing familiar faces calmed me immediately. During the commercial break in the top half hour, I was hustled out and miked up, and over walked Katie Couric. She shook my hand warmly and managed to put me at ease. A producer ran up and gave the backward count.

Katie did a brief preview of my story, with bits and pieces from the *Dateline* segment, before welcoming me to the show. She was the biggest surprise I could have imagined. The interview lasted about eight minutes, which is an eon in morning television, but I got through it without stumbling. After they yelled "Cut," Katie leaned forward, gave me a hug, and started chatting with me about our alma mater and the case. Our rapport was easy and warm, and I sheepishly told her how much I had dreaded talking to her, and how wrong I had been. On the way out to the street, Mike and I ran into Al Roker, who remarked what a powerful piece it was. "I have daughters, you know. So, thank you. Really."

That was a good day.

The following evening, Mike, my mother-in-law, and I gathered to watch *Dateline*. I was glad it was late enough that Ava was already in bed. We sat and patiently watched Ann Curry lead in with the story and then it began. We were transfixed. They had pieced together a fascinating story, which unfolded like a mystery. I had the sense I would have really enjoyed it if it had been someone else's story. But it was my own, and it felt totally bizarre watching it on national television. Of course, though I had worked closely with John, Edie, and the crew, I had little power over how the final piece came out. Beebe had been dubbed the "12-Step rapist," though to me, the AA angle was irrelevant. Someone who apologizes for committing rape in step 9 of an AA program, making amends, still committed that rape. Still, I understood on some level that the 12-Step angle made for good television, and I couldn't control how Beebe was portrayed. I certainly couldn't control how audiences would react. Mike went to the MSNBC

117

Web site, where there was a voting mechanism set up and the question: "Did Liz Seccuro do the right thing by calling the police?" At the end of the day, 81 percent voted yes.

I read a lot of comments—and later, blog posts and e-mails—offering support and comfort. I heard from hundreds of survivors of sexual assault, both male and female, whose stories often overwhelmed me with grief. I heard from women of all ages, men with daughters, people who belonged to AA and felt Beebe had misused step 9. I also got messages from childhood friends, my high school teachers, and former classmates from UVA. It was wonderful to reconnect, and their words touched me deeply.

But not all the responses were positive. Some were thoughtless, others unbelievably cruel. There were those who wrote in to say, "I wouldn't want to be her friend," or "No one deserves to be raped BUT why was she at that party?" There were others who accused me of just wanting attention. Christians who thought I should burn in hell for not turning the other cheek suggested that I should have been home reading my Bible and not off at some "sin-infested" fraternity party and that the Lord wanted for me to be raped to teach me a lesson about the "consequences of evil liquor." I was called a "liberal," a "neo-Con Bushie," a WASP, a Jew, a Republican, a Democrat, a bitch, a slut, and a whore.

Some thought that since I had a marriage and a job now, I should be "thankful." Some thought I was getting justice because I was blonde. Some suggested I should be raped again and more than one threatened to track me down and kill me in graphic ways.

Although some of the responses left me terrified, there was no turning back now. I tried to focus on the positive responses, and told myself that I was making things easier for all the other survivors. My next stop on the press tour was *The Abrams Report*, the show hosted by MSNBC's chief legal correspondent, Dan Abrams. Dan was exactly my age, and a graduate of Duke University. His program was a favorite of those following the big stories of criminal justice, and during this time rape allegations at Duke University were very much in the news. I loved his "Rebuttal" segment, which aired the day after my interview. He swiped back at viewers who had written in with the same kind of e-mails that I had been getting, and he said things I wished I could say.

There followed interviews with various newspapers, *People* magazine, and with Paula Zahn on CNN. I was getting slightly more comfortable with the exposure, but some of the responses only became more frightening.

One morning, I went to the mailbox to find a plain white envelope, addressed to me with a local postmark. Inside was a crudely photocopied photograph of a man holding his erect penis. Letters cut from a magazine spelled out "I hope I'm better than he was." His face was not pictured. We called the Greenwich police, who handled the mail with tweezers and bagged it in an evidence sleeve. They promised to send it to the crime lab, but we never heard another word about it. Truth is, mail is handled by many people and fingerprints are nearly impossible to lift. A week later, I received a photograph of a birthday cake with garish pink and green flowers. Instead of "Happy Birthday," the cake had the inscription "I'm Sorry I Raped You" in childish frosting script. There was only more to come.

The preliminary hearing was looming, where I would have to testify against Beebe and face him for the first time. The media attention multiplied in spades.

CHAPTER 8 *The Preliminary Hearing and Direct Examination*

As the investigation continued, we were told that March 24, 2006, was the date for the preliminary hearing. At one of these sessions testimony is given by witnesses, cross-examination is done by the defense team, and a judge decides whether there is enough evidence against the arrested party for him or her to go to trial. Essentially, it was the big dance, the day they would decide if Beebe's charges would stick.

I was the only person called to testify. Technically my role in the hearing was as a witness; my evidence would determine whether the state had a case. Claude Worrell prepared me as well as he could via telephone and e-mail. He was my lifeline, and I felt very close to him over time. He had an easy and gentle way with me, without sugar-coating the reality of what was to come. Rounding out my support group was my victim advocate, Cherri Murphy, who tended to the emotional realities of what would happen in court. I placed my trust in both of them completely.

A few days prior to the hearing, I got a call from Worrell. His cousin had died and he needed to travel to the funeral. It would occur on the date of the hearing. He said that I had a choice—either we could continue the case until Worrell, the Court, and

I were all available, which could take months, or I could have his colleague Dave Chapman sit with me and argue for the Commonwealth. At first I felt completely defeated. I had never met Chapman and I couldn't imagine going through the hearing without Worrell by my side. What if Chapman wasn't prepared? How could he be? Worrell and I had logged almost daily phone calls and e-mails over the course of months, and Dave had his own caseload. But the idea of waiting was just as untenable. We had psyched ourselves up for so long that postponing was completely out of the question.

"Let's go ahead. Let's do it with Dave," I said.

"Okay then," said Worrell. "I will make certain Dave is briefed."

Mike and I traveled to Charlottesville two days before the hearing. We had arranged for his mother to stay with Ava, to keep her routine as intact as possible. When it was time to go, I hugged her about eighty times. I had packed framed photos of her in my suitcase, and I left her with my well-worn pashmina shawl, which comforted her because it carried my scent. Armed with bottles of water and about ten magazines, I tried to distract myself through the flight. I was cheered knowing that several of my sorority sisters were driving into Charlottesville from all around Virginia to support me.

Chapman and Worrell had both insisted to me that the preliminary hearing was really just a formality, but I was no fool. I knew that testifying and being cross-examined for the first time would be gut-wrenching. Also, since I had been a minor at the time the crime was committed, the hearing was being held in juvenile and domestic relations court, a tiny building where I would have to sit only eight feet from the defendant. I had been expecting to get a lot of preparation for my testimony, but Chapman explained that credible, well-spoken witnesses generally aren't prepped—lawyers don't want the testimony to seem rehearsed. He simply wanted me to come by midmorning the day before to listen to the statement I had made to Detectives Rudman and Godfrey on December 10 and refresh my memory. Mike decided to ride over there with me. He had never really heard the full story. I warned him that it might not be easy to hear.

A staffer led us to an empty office, popped an audio CD into a computer, and left us in private to listen to the recording. As my full account of the rape played, Mike looked forlorn, suddenly smaller in his clothes. Alone in that office, we just sat and listened.

The next day, at about five thirty A.M., I awoke in earnest after a mostly sleepless night. Mike snored peacefully beside me. The day was dawning cloudy and rainy as I made my way to our kitchenette to brew some coffee. On second thought, I decided to go over to the hotel lobby in the main building and grab some coffee there, so I could get a newspaper. On third thought, I slipped on running clothes and grabbed a bottle of water, thinking a run around the bucolic Grounds would help me feel relaxed and strong. I tied on my running shoes and grabbed my iPod on my way down the stairs and out the door. The smell of the oncoming Virginia spring is something I will never forget about that day. It was intense, green, and just gorgeous, despite the clouds. A smile crept across my face. Ambling across the street,

I decided that I'd like a coffee before my run after all, and when I approached the front desk, I stopped dead in my tracks because there, on the front page of the paper was his face. I picked up first the *Daily Progress* and then the *Richmond Times Dispatch*, both of which blared headlines about the day's hearing. That face was the same. The clerks looked at me with knowing eyes and one wished me luck. I skipped the run and headed back up to our suite, juggling coffee, water, and papers.

Mike was still sleeping, but I flipped on the television. "Today, William Nottingham Beebe and his accuser, Liz Seccuro, will meet for the first time in court as a judge will hear evidence in the rape case against Beebe at a preliminary hearing. Seccuro is expected to testify today. If the evidence is found to be sufficient, the case will go to a grand jury for indictment."

Pan to Beebe's mug shot, photos of his arraignment, and him in his striped jumpsuit. He looked just like the man who raped me. He was the man who raped me. My mouth was like a desert, my head pounded, and my ears were hot. I could not feel my hands and feet. They were dead and cold.

"Mike, wake up, honey, please! Mike! Pssst! Wake up—it's on the morning news!" I pleaded.

"Whaaaa?"

"Just wake up and watch this with me," I hissed. I was freaked out.

He rolled over and rubbed his eyes. They about burst from the sockets.

"Oh my God. The case is on television!" he bellowed.

"Um, well, yeah," I said. "I've been trying to tell you this.

I guess it's a big story here. Maybe we should just hide out here all day so no one hassles us."

"Hassles us for what? We didn't do anything. He did." Mike was right. But aside from hiding, I didn't really know what to do until the hearing. We drove to a nearby shopping center to browse books, grab lunch, and kill some time.

Back at the hotel, I put on my courtroom outfit, which consisted of opaque black tights, a black tank top, a black knit skirt, and a pink wool jacket. I wanted to seem businesslike, but not overly somber. Pink was the color of my foundation's logo, and my visiting sorority sisters had pledged to wear it, too, in a show of solidarity. As I dressed in the hotel bathroom, I laughed to myself as I was reminded of one of Ava's favorite movies, *The Incredibles*. There is a scene when a character wants to morph into his superhero self and yells to his wife, *"Where . . . is . . . my . . . supersuit?!"* I was transforming myself into a superwitness. I donned all of the lucky jewelry my husband had given me over the years and tucked my St. Christopher medal into my shoe. It was the same medal I had hidden in my sock as I pushed to deliver Ava, and that had gone rather quickly and without much drama. I knew St. Chris would keep me safe from Beebe.

And then it was time and we could not turn back. That mug shot would be in court, alive and breathing, all six foot-whatever of him. In our rental car, we tooled our way past the Rotunda, Madison Bowl, Phi Kappa Psi, and the Corner. All the years fell away. The plan had been to walk over to the court with Dave Chapman, but Dave had seen the phalanx of cameras, lights, booms, talking heads, and microphones outside the courthouse and called my cell phone. He directed us to meet him there and park in back. We were escorted to the back door under armed guard. Mike gave me a brief hug and Cherri, my victim advocate, held my hand as we entered the room. The courtroom was much smaller than I'd imagined, and this gave me a bit of a start. All was quiet. I was last to arrive—clearly it had been orchestrated that way so that Beebe and I would not run into each other. I sat next to Dave at a long table. At a second table, facing us, were the lovely, raven-haired defense attorney, Rhonda Quagliana; her tall, white-haired boss, Francis McQ. Lawrence; and, of course, the accused. Not eight feet across from me, facing me square, was William Beebe. His face was completely blank and without any emotion. The gallery to my right was filled to capacity. So close were my sorority sisters and husband that I could have touched them if I'd stretched out my right arm. The judge, Edward J. DeBerry, sat to the left at the front of the room on a riser. I was marginally aware of armed guards and bailiffs positioned at every corner of the room, as well as members of the media and garden variety looky-loos who love to see a good session in court, especially in a potentially spectacular rape trial. This was "go" time.

MARCH 24, 2006

THE COURT: We're here this afternoon on the case of William Beebe. Is the Commonwealth ready?

DAVE CHAPMAN: Yes, sir.

THE COURT: Defense ready?

RHONDA QUAGLIANA: Yes, Your Honor.

THE COURT: Okay, let the record reflect the Commonwealth is here in the presence of Mr. Chapman, Commonwealth's Attorney. Defendant is present with his attorneys, Mr. Lawrence and Ms. Quagliana. Are there any witnesses in this case?

CHAPMAN: Yes, there are.

THE COURT: Okay, if they'll come forward, please, and be sworn.

I was the only witness. Knees shaking, I smoothed my knit skirt and put one foot in front of the other in order to be sworn in.

CHAPMAN: Judge, we had intended to call Detective Scott Godfrey, Charlottesville Police Department, to establish venue in the case. And in speaking with Ms. Quagliana, for the purposes of this hearing, venue will be stipulated, so we'll have one witness to present today.

THE COURT: Okay [to me], raise your right hand.

I did.

THE COURT: Okay, if you'll identify yourself for the reporter, please.

ME: Elizabeth Seccuro.

I swore to tell the truth, the whole truth, and nothing but the truth.

THE COURT: Okay, if you'll just have a seat. Mr. Beebe, we
will read the charge to you. Since this is a
preliminary hearing on a felony, no plea need be
entered. It is charged that on or about October
the 5th, 1984, you did unlawfully and
feloniously, in violation of Section 18.2-61 of the
Code of Virginia, commit rape by having sexual
intercourse with E.S., born 12.23.1966, a
seventeen year old juvenile. Such act was
accomplished against the victim's will by force,
threat or intimidation, or against the victim or
another person.

At this time, there was a brief discussion that no media
outside normal court reporting would be allowed to tape
the proceedings. Both prosecution and defense waived opening statements. It was my turn. I had to remain seated next
to Dave Chapman at the conference table, facing William
Beebe and his team, while Chapman's direct examination of
me began.

CHAPMAN: We will call Ms. Seccuro as a witness. Is your name
Elizabeth Seccuro?

ME: Yes, it is.

CHAPMAN: Okay. Now, because we're making a recording of the proceedings today, we'll ask you to keep your voice up to make sure it's picked up on the recording device and to make sure we're all able to hear you.

ME: Okay.

Dave asked me some basic questions, establishing that I was seventeen years old at the time of the alleged crime, living in Charlottesville, a student at the university. He asked whether I was aware of fraternity rush events going on that first semester, and about the nature of my relationship to Jim Long, the friend with whom I'd attended the party. Then, he turned to the night in question.

CHAPMAN: All right. At some point in the early part of October, did you receive a request from him [Jim] about a rush activity?

ME: Yes, I did. On the evening of October 5th he requested that I accompany him to a rush party at the Phi Kappa Psi house.

CHAPMAN: Had you intended to go to any particular activities on that night?

ME: No, I had not.

CHAPMAN: Can you remember what day of the week that would have been?

ME: It was a Thursday.

CHAPMAN: Did you know where that [Phi Kappa Psi] was located?

ME: I may have; I'm not quite sure.

CHAPMAN: Did you actually go somewhere with him?

ME: Yes.

CHAPMAN: About what time of day was it on that day that you went?

ME: I believe it to have been around eleven P.M.

CHAPMAN: Okay. Now let me, to insure the Judge and we are all able to understand where you're describing, with reference to nearby landmarks, could you tell the Court where the Phi Kappa Psi house is?

ME: Yes, it is—if Madison Bowl is a rectangle, the Phi Kappa Psi house is the large house at the, well, at the head—at the head facing the Rotunda direction.*

CHAPMAN: Do you know if at the time, for example, that you went there if you knew anybody who resided in that house or was a member of it?

ME: I did not know anybody who resided in the house. I did know one member vaguely.

---

* Ellipsis points (. . .) used in original court documents to indicate pauses in speech have been changed to em-dashes (—) for reader clarity.

CHAPMAN: When you got there, could you describe what
        activities were ongoing, if any?

ME: The party was in full swing. There was certainly drinking,
there was music, there was foosball, there was just general
socialization.

CHAPMAN: Where were those kinds of activities taking place?

ME: In the first floor, all the common areas.

He asked me about how much beer I'd had to drink, asking
me to indicate the size of the cup with my hands. He asked
whether I knew anyone else at the party, and my relationship to
Hudson Millard. He asked when Jim had left my side, and I explained how the brothers in the house had invited him to smoke.
Then, he asked about the green drink.

CHAPMAN: Can you recall to any extent the taste of it, the
        flavor of it and tell us whether it contained alcohol
        to your knowledge, or—

ME: I assumed it did. It tasted very tart, very lime, and sour—
very sour. Sour in a citrusy way.

CHAPMAN: Now you say you assumed it contained alcohol?

ME: I did—

CHAPMAN: Okay. Did you know?

ME: No, I do not.

CHAPMAN: Did you know if it contained any other substances besides alcohol?

ME: I do not.

CHAPMAN: At the time you got the [green] drink, before consuming any of it, how would you describe how you felt?

ME: I was not intoxicated. I was—I don't know the term for it, but relaxed. Pleasantly relaxed. Not impaired.

CHAPMAN: Now, once you began to drink the drink that you had been given on the second floor, did the way you felt change in any way?

ME: It did.

CHAPMAN: Could you describe how it changed and over what time period that change took place?

ME: Almost with immediacy, but I don't believe I was really attuned or alarmed by it, and over the next fifteen minutes I noticed that my limbs were—the best way to put it was they were sort of immobilized. They felt rubbery. Like a marionette, like they weren't moving very well. It was my arms and legs.

CHAPMAN: The feeling that you're describing, could you describe its onset and progression in terms of whether it was quick or gradual?

ME: It was very quick. It was not the sort of thing you would notice unless you stood up. It was much more marked on just—during my interactions there, just standing or sitting, it became most apparently obvious upon standing.

CHAPMAN: Now, were you moving about after you got the drink and—

ME: I was.

CHAPMAN: In what way and what places and what were you doing?

ME: I was in that room and just socializing with various people, making small talk. At times I was seated on furniture, at times I was standing.

And then:

CHAPMAN: Now, at that time did you know a William Beebe[?]

ME: I did not.

CHAPMAN: Let me ask you to look across the courtroom. The gentleman who's seated between Ms. Quagliana and Mr. Lawrence—

ME: That is him.

CHAPMAN: Did you see that gentleman that night on the second floor?

ME: I did.

CHAPMAN: When did you see him in comparison to the drink that you got on the second floor?

ME: I don't know when he came to be in that room, but I recall an awareness of him being there because we began to speak, so I don't know exactly where he came from.

CHAPMAN: Could you describe to the Court the initial interaction that you had with him?

ME: It was very brief small talk, hi, how are you, introductions, where are you from, what's your major, the sort of thing that you talk about when you meet somebody and are chatting at a party.

More questions followed about our conversation, Beebe's level of intoxication, and my impairment at this point.

CHAPMAN: Now, to what extent do you think, and if you're able to say, you were affected in terms of your ability to see and hear and speak?

ME: I was fine there. I could see very clearly.

CHAPMAN: Do you recall whether you remarked to anybody, to the Defendant or anyone else about how you felt?

ME: I don't recall.

CHAPMAN: In the area you've described on the second floor, was there ever any physical contact between yourself and the Defendant?

ME: Yes, there was.

CHAPMAN: Can you remember what you were doing and how that happened?

ME: While we were talking, we were sitting and he said to me, "I want to show you something," and he grabbed me by my arm and led me down a hallway towards a room.

CHAPMAN: Now, how did that strike you and in light of your awareness or lack of awareness of him, and the context at the time, would you tell the Court how you felt and what you thought and what you did?

ME: It struck me as bizarre because I didn't know this person, but at this point in time, I was really not able to do much for myself, and I thought the best place to be when my friend came back was to be in this room so he could find me. I found it awkward and I found it socially bizarre.

CHAPMAN: Did you go?

ME: I did.

CHAPMAN: Did you offer any physical resistance?

ME: I did, yes.

CHAPMAN: In what way[?]

ME: In my own limited capacity, I know that I said something like "No, I don't want to go" and it was something like "Oh, come on, it'll be fun, let me show you this" and I pretty much good naturedly went along. But I was trying to resist, but not—certainly didn't think anything dangerous was happening.

CHAPMAN: And where did you go ultimately?

ME: To a room at the end of the hall.

Chapman asked for a lot of specifics about the room: position of the room in relation to the street, the bed in relation to the room, the sofa in relation to the door, and the orientation of furniture. This was simply a reiteration of my conversations with Detectives Rudman and Godfrey, where I had drawn a picture of the whole house and of the room in question.

CHAPMAN: Thank you. Now, having gone to that room, could you tell the Court what happened after going into the room?

ME: At this time, the Defendant—there was also a chair and a desk—the Defendant brought me into the room, led me by the arm. He sat down on a chair and he had me—he grabbed me around my waist and hoisted me onto his lap at which time he showed me a book which I recall was bound in the green fabric like—almost like a rare book, an antique book, when they used to actually bind books with cloth. And it was some sort of book of poetry, I don't recall what it was and he began reading it to me and holding me onto his lap and then he began kissing me and I did not really think this was appropriate.

CHAPMAN: What did you do, if anything?

ME: I tried to get up and I did manage to free myself from his grasp and I went out into the hallway as quickly as possible and the room where my handbag was locked from the outside with a padlock.

CHAPMAN: And what did you do, if anything, having reached this point?

Here I started to falter, but there was no going back. I had to walk through the fire and I was acutely aware of Beebe sitting *right there*. I looked to the right a bit to see the comforting faces of people I knew. They all looked stricken. Up until this point it had been as if I was speaking of someone else during my testimony. But the image of that room being padlocked on the outside made me fight back tears. I felt all of the defeat and helplessness rushing back. Plus, I knew where we were going with this line of questioning. I felt myself sliding down the rabbit hole.

ME: I began to kick and scream because I knew that my acquaintance, Mr. Millard, was locked in that room.

CHAPMAN: Okay, had you seen that happen?

ME: I saw them usher him into the room and lock him in there.

CHAPMAN: Now, did you—did the door come open at any time?

ME: No, it did not.

CHAPMAN: Were you able to contact anyone?

ME: I just began screaming and kicking the door. I had a flat shoe on. I was pounding the door, I was calling Hud's name. I said that I wanted to leave and could he help me, that my purse was in there, could he help me?

CHAPMAN: Was there any response from inside?

ME: No, there was not.

You could hear an audible sigh of resignation in the room. No one wanted to go any further here, least of all me.

CHAPMAN: Was there any response from anybody else in the vicinity?

ME: There was. One of the brothers, who ostensibly had been mixing drinks in the room on the second floor, came over to me as I was pounding and kicking and screaming on the door. He picked me up under my shoulders, and the Defendant grabbed me from behind and deposited me back into the Defendant's room.

CHAPMAN: Now, and where were you taken?

ME: I was deposited back into that same room overlooking Madison Lane.

CHAPMAN: And who was in that room after that happened?

ME: The Defendant.

There, in the room, with my rapist. And here I was, in a room, facing him again.

CHAPMAN: Was there anybody else in the room?

ME: No.

CHAPMAN: Where did the other person go, if you know?

ME: He left.

CHAPMAN: Now, let me ask you, as of the time that you were deposited back into the room, would you tell the Court how you were feeling physically and, as well, how you were feeling in terms of your alertness and sobriety and the like?

ME: I can tell you that I was extremely alert. I could see, I could hear, I could speak. However, my muscle coordination was extremely compromised. I can also tell you that I was having a bit of difficulty breathing, most likely because I was very panicky at this stage.

CHAPMAN: Now, was anybody making physical contact with you after you ended up back in the room?

ME: The Defendant.

CHAPMAN: Okay, what was the physical contact that he was making with you after you got put back in the room?

ME: Well, he shut the door and he turned out the lights. And I knew it was him because the lights were on.

CHAPMAN: Now, as those things happened, were you in physical contact with him?

ME: I came to be, yes.

It made me nervous breaking this down into second-by-second detail. It all happened so suddenly, a rush in my memory, and I feared that the defense would use it against me if there was a hole of even a few seconds in my story.

CHAPMAN: Now, when you came to be, yes, the way I'm hearing that is there was a period of time when you were not in physical contact with him.

ME: I was still trying to get away, one last effort. When I mean I came to be, I mean there was a few seconds interval.

CHAPMAN: And what was the physical contact that he was having with you?

ME: He was holding me by my left arm and he proceeded to very swiftly take my clothes off.

CHAPMAN: Okay, now, let me ask you, are you the same approximate size now as you were then?

ME: Yes.

CHAPMAN: How tall are you now?

ME: I'd like to think five-seven, but I believe it's five six and a half.

CHAPMAN: And are you the same approximate weight now as you were then?

ME: Give or take.

CHAPMAN: In comparison with yourself would you describe the Defendant's size at that time?

ME: He seemed extremely large and tall to me and I had flat shoes on at the time, unlike today. He—my sense was that he was a big guy.

CHAPMAN: Could you describe the force with which you were held at that time?

ME: It was not comfortable. It was extremely forceful.

CHAPMAN: To what extent were you able to move or free yourself or the like?

ME: I wasn't—I was not able to.

I started to cry.

CHAPMAN: Now, you describe your clothes having been removed, could you tell the Court what you recall you were wearing at that time?

ME: Yes, I was wearing a denim miniskirt, a Guess miniskirt with a snap closure and a zip. I was wearing a long sleeved crew neck cotton sweater with pink, pale blue, yellow and white squares. A bra, underpants, navy blue leather flat shoes, a string of pearls and pearl stud earrings.

Even after burning those clothes, I would never forget them.

CHAPMAN: Now, could you describe to the Judge how it is the Defendant was able to remove your clothing under the circumstances?

ME: In what order, or—

CHAPMAN: If you can remember the order, and if you can remember physically what he did, please describe those things.

ME: If I'm him and you are me [Dave remained seated during the questioning, and he and I are sitting next to one another], I was held by—that would be my left arm, whereupon he unsnapped and unzipped my skirt and hooked his finger into my underwear and that came off all at once. Seconds later, the sweater came off over my head, it was a pullover, and seconds later, he unhooked my bra.

CHAPMAN: Could you describe when you say he threw you onto the bed, what is it he did, where is it you ended up and how rapidly or slowly and with what degree of force, if any, did those occur?

We had reached the moment—the actual crime. I could hear a bit of a sharp breath from the gallery and saw, out of my right eye, my husband start to slowly rock back and forth.

ME: It was rather forceful. Mind you, my arms and legs are not really coordinated, so it didn't take very long. It was a very swift motion. My head ended up at the, for lack of a better word, north end, probably the north end of the room where the pillow would be and my feet ended up at the foot of the bed.

CHAPMAN: Where was he?

ME: He was right there.

CHAPMAN: Standing, sitting, what—can you describe that?

ME: In a matter of moments he was climbing on top of me.

CHAPMAN: Do you know whether he had his clothes on?

ME: Yes, his clothes were on.

CHAPMAN: Did he remove his clothing?

ME: No, he did not.

CHAPMAN: At any time did he remove his clothing?

ME: Not to my recollection[.]

CHAPMAN: Would you tell the Judge what he did?

ME: Help me out here. Where do you want me to start?

CHAPMAN: Well, you've described that he was on top of you?

ME: Yes.

CHAPMAN: At that time he was on top of you, what was going on? What did he do?

ME: The first thing that I recall is that I was digitally penetrated with his hand.

CHAPMAN: What part of your body was digitally penetrated?

ME: My vagina.

CHAPMAN: Could you tell the Court what he did in order to be able to do that, with what force, if any, he was able to accomplish that?

ME: It was rather forceful I recall because it was extraordinarily painful for me. And it was quite brief, ten seconds, I guess that's not very brief when that is happening.

CHAPMAN: Were you penetrated in any other way or by any other object?

ME: Yes.

CHAPMAN: Would you describe that to the Court, please?

ME: After the digital penetration, he lay on top of me and forced his penis in and around my vaginal area. I say around because there—how do I say this—?

CHAPMAN: Well, use your own words and describe what he did.

ME: Okay. He was extremely forceful and because I was a virgin, there was—he was having a very difficult time penetrating me, so he was being extremely aggressive and fast and rough.

Mike started to become visibly and audibly agitated and I feared he would jump the seats and strangle William Beebe. A bailiff came over, bent down and whispered to him to settle down or he would have to leave the courtroom.

ME: I remember the first thing I tried to do was to keep my legs together in the hopes that he wouldn't get in as hard as he got. And I remember having my hands up over my face. It's almost like when a turtle is on its back and he can't—and it's fighting, but it really is not getting anywhere. My arms then became pinned to my sides by the Defendant, so my arms were no longer fighting, so I tried to move my legs, to kick my legs, but once again, he was just—he was just so much bigger than me, and I couldn't.

Sobbing.

CHAPMAN: Could you tell the Court if there were any other ways in which you resisted what he was attempting to do?

ME: I said "No!" I said "Get off me!" I said "Please stop, you're hurting me!"

CHAPMAN: Did he do that.

ME: No, he did not.

CHAPMAN: How did it stop?

ME: I don't know how it stopped because after a few minutes, I—I remember looking out the window, which was to my left, I remember seeing the streetlight and wondering—I don't know if the window was open or closed, wondering if anyone could hear me. And I—I just—I remember thinking "I'm going to die here in this room and my mom and dad aren't going to find me." And all the while, the rape was continuing and, at that point, I lost consciousness.

CHAPMAN: Now, when you say you lost consciousness, is that something of which you're aware of [or] is it something in the nature of a conclusion that you reached based on other things?

ME: No, I literally remember just everything—I remember seeing stars from the pain and it became too great for me and I recall just saying, "You know, it's okay, you can just let go, you can—you can go to sleep." And I just blacked out. I actually remember the process of it.

The worst was over.

CHAPMAN: Can you remember the next thing? What's your first recollection after that?

ME: I awoke on the sofa, which was perpendicular to the bed where the attack occurred. And I was naked and wrapped in a sheet which had blood on it.

CHAPMAN: Where did it have blood on it?

ME: Sort of where—I had been wrapped in it, I don't know how. And it was—there was sort of a one and a half foot square area around my mid-section after I inspected the sheet. No one was in the room when I awoke.

CHAPMAN: Do you know how much later it was that you awoke or became conscious?

ME: I do not recall. It was early morning, approximately.

CHAPMAN: How do you know it was early morning, and if you have a time estimate, would you describe that?

ME: I would describe it about eight A.M. to nine A.M. simply because of the position of the sun and my own internal body clock.

CHAPMAN: Was it light out?

ME: It was.

CHAPMAN: Was it fully light out?

ME: Yes.

CHAPMAN: Was there anybody in the room?

ME: No. May I back up?

CHAPMAN: Is there something you've forgotten or left out?

ME: Yes.

CHAPMAN: What is that?

ME: After I became unconscious, I don't know how much time later, I do recall the door to the room opening, I recall hearing voices. I had a sense that there were people milling about. I had a sense that I was seen there.

CHAPMAN: I'm not sure I've heard you; are you using the word I was "seen" there or I was "seeing" there?

ME: No, I was seen there by others, by people.

CHAPMAN: Can you tell the Court whether that was—well, what were the lighting conditions at the time that you had that observation?

ME: The room was dark as it had been during the attack. And when the door to the room opened, some light from the hallway was let into the room, so I was obviously aware.

CHAPMAN: Could you describe the lighting conditions outside at that time?

ME: The lights were on in the hallway.

CHAPMAN: But my question was outside of the building. Was it still dark or—

ME: Yes, it was still dark.

CHAPMAN: Now, did you do or say anything at that time?

ME: Not that I recall. I was in shock I recall.

CHAPMAN: Do you have the ability to say who or how many people were there?

ME: No. I do recall there being, from hearing their voices, that it was more than one since there was conversation. But I was unable to speak or cry out and I didn't know if the Defendant was one of those people.

CHAPMAN: Do you know if you had any interaction with any of them?

ME: I don't recall.

CHAPMAN: Do you know if you moved in a significant way?

ME: I may have tried to, but significant, no.

CHAPMAN: Now, after the time period when you're aware it was fully light outside, did you remain in the room?

ME: No, not for long.

CHAPMAN: Now, while you were still in the room, did you see anybody?

ME: Yes.

CHAPMAN: Who did you see?

ME: The Defendant.

CHAPMAN: Could you describe that to the Court?

ME: Yes. As I was on the sofa, still naked and wrapped in this sheet, he came in, fully clothed, was packing his backpack and somewhat incredulously said "good morning," or something—I—I—you know, I really don't remember exactly what he said. He made some reference to the fact that it was chilly outside, that I would need a jacket. And I just remember thinking this was so completely incongruous. I was standing there with no clothes on and in a sheet and had just been raped and I don't believe I—I don't know if I responded.

Dave led me through the rest of the testimony—finding my clothes, retrieving my handbag, going down the stairs to leave the house.

CHAPMAN: Is the person who did those things to you in Court here today?

ME: Yes, he is.

CHAPMAN: Would you point him out, please?

ME: [I pointed toward the Defendant.]

CHAPMAN: The record—

THE COURT: The record will reflect she's indicated the Defendant.

CHAPMAN: Thank you. Those are the questions that I have. Answer questions from Counsel.

Breathe. Breathe. This part was over.

CHAPTER 9

Cross-Examination and Redirect

I felt relief after getting my testimony out. But there was more to come: the cross-examination. The job of the defense attorney is to make the witness look as confused and untruthful as possible. Rhonda Quagliana was just doing what she was paid to do—I didn't blame her then and harbor no ill will toward her now. But her questioning was far from pleasant.

Rhonda conferred with Francis Lawrence, shuffled her papers, and took a very long pause. She looked perfectly put together, with flawless skin and raven hair, dressed in a black pantsuit and low-heeled pumps. She launched right into the classic blame-the-victim triumvirate of "You were out on a school night," "You drank alcohol," and "You wore a short skirt." If it had not been so painful, it would have been laughable in its predictability. With no jury to impress—or alienate—at these preliminary hearings, the defense attorneys can attack hard.

RHONDA QUAGLIANA: Ms. Seccuro, I'm Rhonda Quagliana.
Did you have Friday class that
semester?

ME: I did.

QUAGLIANA: And did you go to class on Friday?

ME: I did not.

QUAGLIANA: Okay. And—but it's because you have a Friday class that you think this was on a Thursday night, is that correct?

ME: Correct.

QUAGLIANA: And is it fair to say that you had been attending fraternity parties and the like through the semester up until October?

ME: I had been to a few, yes.

QUAGLIANA: And you had consumed alcohol at those parties?

ME: Certainly.

QUAGLIANA: Okay. When you awoke and found yourself in a bloody sheet, was the blood just located on one area of the sheet, or was the sheet covered with blood?

ME: I would say there were about six or seven ovals, two to three inches in diameter.

QUAGLIANA: Okay, and you were naked at this point?

ME: I was.

QUAGLIANA: And was there blood on other parts of your body besides the area between your legs?

ME: I was going to say in between my legs.

QUAGLIANA: Is that the only area that any blood ever touched?

ME: Yes.

QUAGLIANA: And where was the bloody area between your legs?

ME: Well, there was some dried blood on my inner thighs.

QUAGLIANA: Okay, how far down your legs did that go?

ME: Almost to my knees.

QUAGLIANA: What area of your legs did it cover?

ME: I'm not sure I get your meaning.

QUAGLIANA: I'm sorry. Was it—

ME: But I just answered that.

QUAGLIANA: Thank you. If it went down to your knees—

ME: The inside, the inside of my thighs.

QUAGLIANA: The inside, you know, did it cover—what area did it cover around the inside of your legs?

ME: Maybe like a two inch, is that what you're looking for?

QUAGLIANA: Yes, that's what I want to know.

ME: Two inch—two inch wide area.

These questions had the intended effect of making me nervous about the details of my answers—focusing on minutiae, and especially the traumatic minutiae of the blood.

QUAGLIANA: Was your jewelry intact?

ME: Yes.

QUAGLIANA: And you testified that the stripping of your clothes occurred all in one area, is that correct, one area of the room?

ME: Yes.

QUAGLIANA: And that Mr. Beebe had your arm while he was taking your clothes off?

ME: One arm and then the other.

QUAGLIANA: Okay. Oh, he had one arm and then the other? When did he take your other arm?

ME: The sweater. No, no, no, to take my sweater off, he began by holding my left arm and then to take the other arm out, switched arms.

QUAGLIANA: Okay.

ME: I'm sorry if I was unclear.

QUAGLIANA: That's okay. Well, I'm trying to find out. So, and you testified that he was holding you very forcefully with his hand, is that correct?

ME: Correct.

QUAGLIANA: And when you went to retrieve your clothes that morning, your clothing was right in that area where he had allegedly stripped your clothes off, is that correct?

As if to say that in a rape, clothing must be strewn wildly about the room.

ME: Correct.

QUAGLIANA: And you recovered everything except your underwear?

ME: Correct.

QUAGLIANA: Okay. And you testified that you were wearing a denim miniskirt, is that correct?

ME: Yes.

QUAGLIANA: And, if you could just tell me, how—what was the length of the skirt? How far down did it go?

What? Really? I felt the same swell of anger I had felt when I screamed at my mother for asking about my clothes that day in the dean's office.

ME: What are you implying? I would say that it went to mid-thigh. Would you like me to stand up and demonstrate for you?

She ignored my hate-dripping sarcasm.

QUAGLIANA: Sure, thank you.

So I stood.

ME: The skirt I'm currently wearing—

THE COURT: If the Witness would please step forward just so the Court and the Court Reporter can see.

ME: About two to three inches shorter than the hem I'm currently wearing.

QUAGLIANA: Okay. You—I take it that before—this is sort of a dumb question, but before you left the room, you put on the clothes that you could find, correct?

ME: Yes.

QUAGLIANA: Including your shoes, is that right?

ME: Yes.

QUAGLIANA: And you would testify that your foot had been injured the night before from having to try to kick the door down where your friend Hudson was, is that correct?

ME: Correct.

QUAGLIANA: And your toe had already, according to your account, begun to swell, is that right?

ME: Yes.

QUAGLIANA: And would you say you had trouble getting your feet into your shoes?

ME: I had trouble getting my right foot into my right shoe.

QUAGLIANA: Okay, and was your toe bleeding at that point?

ME: No.

QUAGLIANA: Okay. And when you put on your clothing, and particularly your skirt, did your skirt make contact with any blood, if you know?

ME: I stepped into it, so I'm not quite sure.

QUAGLIANA: Did you have other opportunities during the morning to examine yourself to ascertain your condition after this occurred?

ME: Certainly.

QUAGLIANA: Okay, and did you see any blood on your clothing?

ME: After sitting—subsequently sitting, that, yeah, there was a bit on the hem on the back.

QUAGLIANA: Okay. And tell me what injuries you would say you sustained as a result of this incident?

ME: My toe, which became, you know, just worse later on was most certainly broken and I know this because I was a classical ballerina and I had broken my toes many times. A few of my ribs were bruised. I had a bruise in the back of my head on the center left side and I had a contusion on my right cheekbone.

QUAGLIANA: Were there any other injuries?

ME: There had been—because I photographed them, I do recall just some fingerprints on my arms.

QUAGLIANA: [When] did you photograph your injuries?

ME: I photographed my injuries on Saturday.

QUAGLIANA: And do you still have those photographs?

ME: I do not.

QUAGLIANA: Okay, who did you show them to, if anybody?

ME: I didn't take the photographs. My friend, who came down from D.C., took them. I showed them—I'm not sure who I showed them to.

QUAGLIANA: How long did you have the photographs after this incident occurred?

ME: For quite some years. I believe I lost track of them during my first marriage.

What I would give for those pictures now!

QUAGLIANA: How many photographs were there?

ME: I'm not sure.

QUAGLIANA: Was it a stack or two or three?

ME: No, it was not a stack. No, it was more like four or five photos.

QUAGLIANA: Okay. Was there anything damaged with regard to your mouth.

ME: No, not that I recall.

QUAGLIANA: And when you say you had a contusion on your cheek, what did that look like?

ME: It merely looked like a small bruise and it was visible, but easily covered up with makeup.

QUAGLIANA: Okay. And when you say that there were fingerprints on your arm, what did that look like?

ME: They looked like blue bruises. They looked like fingerprints.

QUAGLIANA: And was that on one arm or on both arms?

ME: There were more on my right arm than on my left arm.

QUAGLIANA: Okay. Was any of your clothing torn?

ME: No.

QUAGLIANA: Were you having your menstrual period during this time?

ME: I was not.

QUAGLIANA: Okay. And when you left the house, I think you testified that it was daylight and about eight A.M., is that correct?

ME: Between eight and nine to my best recollection.

QUAGLIANA: Okay, could it have been any later than that?

ME: It could have.

QUAGLIANA: But you believe it was sometime prior to, say, noon for sure?

ME: Yes, because I saw people—I saw people on their way to class as I was walking.

QUAGLIANA: And you left the house on the exit that takes you out to Rugby Road, is that correct?

ME: No, I left the house on the exit that takes me to Madison Lane.

QUAGLIANA: Okay. And did you walk down Madison Lane?

DAVE CHAPMAN: Judge, I'm going to object to this scope of the examination. We ceased asking questions upon her exit from the house.

Anything past this point is for the purpose of discovery.

Chapman objected to Quagliana's line of questioning because the scope of the preliminary hearing was to end at the point when I left the Phi Kappa Psi house. It had been agreed that testimony about events after leaving the house would not be introduced until trial.

QUAGLIANA: Judge, it's cross examination and we have broad latitude here. And—and to the extent of the witness' credibility and her memory, this is relevant and we should be allowed to inquire.

THE COURT: I'll sustain the objection.

A small victory. But Rhonda Quagliana had plenty of other questions.

QUAGLIANA: While you were at the house in the bedroom, had the bleeding from your vaginal area stopped?

ME: While I was at the house?

QUAGLIANA: Yes.

ME: It had certainly slowed. There was fresh blood being deposited on the sheet that morning when I awoke, although not much.

QUAGLIANA: And before you left the house, you did not do anything to alter your appearance or clean yourself, or anything of that sort, is that correct?

I stumbled, forgetting to mention my efforts to clean myself in the filthy fraternity bathroom.

ME: No, I did not.

QUAGLIANA: And you didn't do anything to alter your clothing, correct?

ME: No, I did not.

QUAGLIANA: And just to make sure I understand, the sweater that you were wearing was a crewneck sweater, correct?

ME: Quite like the sweater you are wearing under your jacket.

QUAGLIANA: And—and the bra you were wearing, could you just describe that for me, please?

Unreal.

ME: It was a simple white lace bra and my underwear matched it.

QUAGLIANA: You testified that you went to the party with somebody by the name of Jim Long, is that correct?

ME: Correct.

QUAGLIANA: And also there was another student by the name of Hud Millard, is that correct?

ME: [He] was there. I didn't go to the party with Hudson Millard.

QUAGLIANA: I understand. How did you know Mr. Millard?

ME: Many of us first years knew him to be an extremely popular resident advisor. He was a mere—he was a trusted figure on Grounds.

QUAGLIANA: Was he a resident advisor in your dorm or another dorm?

ME: I had seen him from around one of my friends from one of my classes. He was that person's resident advisor. He's a very popular resident advisor. Many people knew him.

QUAGLIANA: But you were on a speaking basis with him?

ME: Yes.

QUAGLIANA: Okay, and he recognized you at the party and you recognized him?

ME: Yes.

QUAGLIANA: And you talked to him at the party?

ME: Yes.

QUAGLIANA: Okay, and when you first arrived at the Phi Psi house that night, did you see other friends from your dorm there?

ME: Yes, correct.

QUAGLIANA: And there were a lot of women in attendance at this party because that's part of the point of rush is to get women to the party, is that correct?

ME: I'm not sure the point of rush. I'm not a fraternity brother.

QUAGLIANA: I'm sorry, I didn't mean to make you speculate about that, but there were certainly a lot of women at the party, correct?

ME: You know, I don't know.

QUAGLIANA: Do you remember seeing any women at the party?

ME: Yes.

QUAGLIANA: You said that when you went upstairs, there were ten or twelve people on the upstairs level, is that correct?

ME: On the second floor level.

QUAGLIANA: And were any of those people women?

ME: Yes.

I didn't know what she was trying to prove, except that if there were other women there, and they didn't get raped, I must have been doing something wrong.

QUAGLIANA: Okay.

ME: May I clarify that point, actually?

QUAGLIANA: Sure.

ME: One of the women that I recognized happened to go up the stairs with me and also went with Jim Long to wherever they went off to.

QUAGLIANA: Who was that?

ME: Her name was Cricket.

QUAGLIANA: Cricket what?

ME: Don't remember her last name.

QUAGLIANA: Was she in your dormitory?

ME: No, she was a friend of Jim's.

QUAGLIANA: How long were you in the upstairs area before the two guys approached you and asked you—was it two guys who approached you and asked you if you wanted something else to drink?

ME: Correct.

QUAGLIANA: Was Mr. Beebe one of those people?

166

ME: No, he was not.

QUAGLIANA: And, in fact, he was not any part of the process by which you received this sort of mystery drink, correct?

ME: Was he tending bar? No.

QUAGLIANA: Well, he wasn't—he didn't have any role in giving you the drink?

ME: No, he did not.

QUAGLIANA: Mix it or serve it or anything, correct?

ME: No, he did not.

She asked again what happened to Jim, to Cricket, to Hud—how I had been left alone. Then we were back to clothing.

QUAGLIANA: Do you recall what Mr. Beebe was wearing that night?

ME: I have a general idea. I have an impression twenty-two years later.

THE COURT: Don't tell us unless you know.

QUAGLIANA: Do you know?

ME: I do know he was wearing a plaid shirt.

QUAGLIANA: Okay, but you recall—you certainly recall what you were wearing, correct?

ME: Yes, I do.

QUAGLIANA: And you even recall what your friend, Jim, was wearing, isn't that true?

ME: Yes.

QUAGLIANA: I mean, you told the police right down to the fact that he was wearing a belt, is that correct?

CHAPMAN: I object to any use of any other statement unless it's for the purpose of impeachment, and the witness has said yes in response to "Do you remember?" So, she has a recollection and she can testify and it doesn't matter what she said to the Police. There's no impeachment at this time. ["Impeachment" means challenging a witness's credibility.]

QUAGLIANA: Do you recall telling the Police that your friend—

CHAPMAN: OBJECTION.

QUAGLIANA: I'm sorry.

CHAPMAN: The same premise.

THE COURT: Miss Quagliana.

QUAGLIANA: Yes, thank you, Your Honor. Do you recall that Mr. Long was wearing a belt?

ME: Yes.

I knew because Jim had asked my opinion on his clothing that night.

QUAGLIANA: Okay. And—but your memory about what Mr. Beebe was wearing is just limited to the shirt, is that correct?

ME: I don't want to answer to exactly what he was wearing unless—I may have the shirt color wrong and I don't want to do that.

QUAGLIANA: And you remember specifically that he was reading to you from a book bound in green fabric?

ME: Correct.

QUAGLIANA: You testified that during the time that you would describe as the rape that you remember a door opening and people milling around. What do you recall about that?

ME: Just that. I remember—I recall—I recall being aware of the presence of others in the room.

QUAGLIANA: So when you testify that you had lost consciousness, were you conscious or unconscious during the course of these events?

ME: At the course of which events?

QUAGLIANA: Well, I mean after—after a certain point you testified that you lost consciousness, but you also say that you remember something about people being there[,] coming in the room, so I'm trying to get an idea of the level of your awareness.

ME: I lost consciousness because the horror of what was happening to me caused me to "check out." I then became conscious again upon hearing the door, hearing voices and seeing light in the room. I then became unconscious again, I assume.

Quagliana flipped through her documents to a new sheet of paper, a newspaper article. She had dug up two articles from student newspapers from my undergrad days. I had mentioned one of these articles to Beebe in an e-mail, which might be how his attorneys found them. Dean Todd had encouraged me to speak about my experience, and I had, under the condition of anonymity, with names and some details changed. Quagliana tried to press me on quotes I'd made back then—to see, I suppose, if my story had changed over time. But neither Chapman nor the judge had seen these articles. I hadn't seen them myself in two decades. The judge became frustrated, and finally Quagliana took a different tack.

QUAGLIANA: You testified in the beginning that you knew the date of this incident because you kept it in a journal, is that correct?

ME: I wrote it down when it happened, yes.

QUAGLIANA: And do you have that journal?

ME: From twenty-two years ago?

QUAGLIANA: Yes, ma'am.

ME: No.

QUAGLIANA: Okay. Did you keep any of the clothing?

ME: I did.

QUAGLIANA: What did you keep?

ME: I kept all the clothing.

QUAGLIANA: And where is it?

ME: I kept all of the clothing for quite some time. When I realized that nothing was going to be done for me, via the University channels, and I don't recall when, at one point I came to burn those—to burn that clothing.

After that line of questioning, my desperate act sounded suspicious.

QUAGLIANA: If I can have a moment, Your Honor. Thank you. Thank you, Your Honor, that's all.

I was relieved when Quagliana sat down. Now it was time for the redirect examination, by Dave Chapman, the Commonwealth's Attorney.

CHAPMAN: Just a couple of questions on redirect. Now, you described having located your clothing in the vicinity where it was removed?

ME: Yes.

CHAPMAN: The things that you located, were they all in that vicinity?

ME: Well, it wasn't a large room, they were scattered on the floor.

CHAPMAN: Okay. Did you have any difficulty locating the things that you did find and put on?

ME: I was in—I don't recall if I did. I just wanted to find them.

CHAPMAN: Well, for example, did you make any special or extra effort to find the underpants that you could not find?

ME: Yes. I got down on the floor and looked under the bed and under the sofa.

CHAPMAN: Could you find them anywhere?

ME: No.

CHAPMAN: Ms. Quagliana asked you about whether any of your clothing was torn or damaged[.] I cannot remember the precise language used, but was any of your clothing affected by the events?

ME: Yes, it was.

CHAPMAN: What clothing and in what way?

ME: My sweater, the crew neck, because it was a cotton/Lycra blend, the hole—the pullover—where you put your head, was stretched out.

CHAPMAN: Were any of the items affected in a way that you observed?

ME: Not when I retrieved them to put them back on.

CHAPMAN: How about upon later inspection, were you able to detect any way in which any of the other items were affected?

ME: Later I—after sitting, I obviously had deposited some blood onto the skirt.

CHAPMAN: Any other [e]ffect that you can recall?

ME: I don't recall.

CHAPMAN: Now, at the time you described becoming aware of the door opening and light and other people being in the room—

ME: Yes.

CHAPMAN: Had the sexual assault been completed by then?

ME: I assume as I was not actively being assaulted at the time. I was—

CHAPMAN: At that time that you became aware of people to the extent you were, was any additional sexual assault or any other kind of contact made with you by those people?

This was the question I had asked Beebe in the e-mail about other assailants.

ME: I don't recall. That is—that remains a question I have.

CHAPMAN: But do you recall any?

ME: No, I do not.

CHAPMAN: Thank you, that's all I have.

THE COURT: Ms. Quagliana.

I almost wished Chapman had had more questions. But now I had to face Quagliana once again. This was the recross-examination.

QUAGLIANA: Was the collar of your shirt visibly stretched out?

ME: To me?

QUAGLIANA: Was it significantly altered?

ME: To me, yes, to the naked eye.

QUAGLIANA: When you testified in response to Mr. Chapman's questions about the presence of others, you have

said on prior occasions that you thought that this
was likely a gang rape, is that correct?

The phrase "gang rape" shot like a bullet through the court-room. There were gasps, then the sound of journalists' pencils scratching furiously. I didn't specifically remember being assaulted by anyone else, but I remembered the voices, the bodies. I had asked the question in an e-mail to Beebe, and he had said he was the only one. I was terrified that there might be more to know. Still, no number of assailants could erase the terror of Beebe's assault from my memory. The horrible possibility did not lessen Beebe's guilt.

CHAPMAN: Objection, objection, absolutely objection! Never said during this examination, not a subject of prior inconsistent statement. Not covered here. I object to that line of questioning.

QUAGLIANA: Mr. Chapman asked her about the presence of other people, and she said that that was an unanswered question for her. And I'm allowed to ask her if she has made statements prior to this inconsistent with what she said here today, and certainly to inquire about a subject that he brought up in his examination. His question was whether or not she—what she could say about the presence of others, and her answer was that she—that that was an unanswered issue for her.

And the idea of what she's described is that there are other people in the room, and I should be allowed to ask her if she thinks other people had sexual contact with her.

THE COURT: I'll allow the question. I think it—

CHAPMAN: Judge, here's— [M]y objection is to the reference of other statements.

THE COURT: Okay, let's delete the point about other statements but let's get to—you can ask her that question.

QUAGLIANA: Do you think there were other people involved?

CHAPMAN: Objection. Her belief in that regard is something quite different from the knowledge or recollection or the like, and I object to that question.

THE COURT: Rephrase the question.

QUAGLIANA: What do you remember about other people being involved?

THE COURT: At what point?

QUAGLIANA: At that point at which you testified that there were other people in the room.

ME: I will answer this the best way I can. Because I had been unconscious, and I recalled other people in the room at some point of the night, because of something I heard subsequently from one of the other brothers that was pledging and because of the fact that I was aware of other people in the room, that is why it remains an unanswered question. The only person I recall assaulting me is—

THE COURT: There is not a question for you right now.

ME: I'm sorry.

QUAGLIANA: Do you recall speaking to Detective Rudman about this matter? A Charlottesville Police Officer?

ME: About which matter specifically?

QUAGLIANA: Well, about the allegation that you're making that Mr. Beebe raped you?

ME: Yes.

QUAGLIANA: Okay. And did you know that your conversation was being recorded?

ME: Yes.

QUAGLIANA: And do you remember telling him that you have a vague recollection of people in the room, perhaps spectators?

ME: Yes.

I was scared of going down this path, and also worried it was a distraction from the charges against Beebe.

QUAGLIANA: And that you may remember other people taking part, but you're not sure, is that what you told Detective Rudman?

ME: That may be what I told him.

QUAGLIANA: And by other people taking part, you mean other people sexually assaulting you, correct?

ME: I mean that in the sense that it was told to me afterwards that that happened, so—in giving my statement, which took a long time—

THE COURT: You've answered the question.

ME: Okay.

QUAGLIANA: Are you saying that information you received from other people after this incident may have influenced what you think happened?

ME: Not with respect to your client.

QUAGLIANA: With respect to anything, including the presence of other people who may have participated in a gang rape?

ME: I know that other people were on the floor. I know that other people were present and were able to open the door because it was not locked.

QUAGLIANA: When were you given this information about other people's presence and who did you talk to about that?

ME: Mere days afterwards.

QUAGLIANA: And who told you about that?

ME: There was a fellow student named Ned Cullen, who was in one of my classes, who was rushing the fraternity.

Ned was a friend whom I'd seen some days later at lunch. He'd sat down and said, "Did you hear about the girl who was gang-raped at Phi Psi?" I jumped, but I didn't know whether that girl was me, or whether some other girl had been assaulted, too. I asked whether he was still planning to rush the house after what had happened. He said, "Of course, my whole family is Phi Kappa Psi, so, what can you do?" But we didn't get to that story.

QUAGLIANA: And what did he tell you?

THE COURT: Now, I think we're getting far afield.

QUAGLIANA: Well, it goes—this is what she's testified to, Your Honor.

THE COURT: No, ma'am, it's not. She did not testify to anything about anybody else assaulting her.

CHAPMAN: And the Commonwealth's objection would be, Your Honor, that if Counsel is attempting to show that her recollection today is influenced by the statement of people, that's one thing. But to simply ask "what did he tell you" sounds to the Commonwealth more like Discovery rather than the appropriate statements that she started out making.

QUAGLIANA: Thank you, Your Honor, that's all.

THE COURT: Anything further from the Commonwealth?

CHAPMAN: No, Your Honor.

THE COURT: Anything from the Defense?

QUAGLIANA: No, Your Honor, thank you.

THE COURT: Motion from the Commonwealth?

CHAPMAN: We'll move to certify.

THE COURT: Argument on certification?

QUAGLIANA: Judge, it's probable cause standard, it's not a high standard, we'll reserve our argument for trial in Circuit Court. Thank you.

Not much of a fight. For now.

I was excused, and Cherri Murphy hustled me out of the courtroom so fast that I didn't even feel my feet touching the ground. I was gone before I could hear the most important words of the day.

THE COURT: Okay the Court does find probabl[e] cause. The case will be certified. What's the next meeting of the Grand Jury?

CHAPMAN: April 17th.

The preliminary hearing was over. The next step was the grand jury and, thankfully, I would not be called as a witness there.

Cherri Murphy had led me back into a holding room, where I was to wait until most of the press had filtered out so I wouldn't be besieged at the door. Mike had followed us out of the courtroom, and when I turned to him he was wild-eyed with anger. I thought he was upset about being in the same room as Beebe, or upset, as I was, by Rhonda Quagliana's questions.

"How could you?!" he screamed at me.

I had not imagined his anger would be directed at me.

"You tripped up! You let that bitch rattle you! What the hell were you thinking? You forgot so many things!"

I had failed. After we had been through so much together, preparing for this moment. On some level, I felt he was right—there were questions I could have answered better, incriminating details I had left out. But he couldn't understand how wrecked I felt, under pressure and sitting so close to my attacker.

I began to cry. Then I felt angry, too. I started to lunge toward my husband. Cherri Murphy came between us. "You two, this happens, this happens. But this can destroy you. Do not let it destroy you. You've come so, so far. It hurts. It's awful, but you love one another and now is not the time to divide. She did it. She's survived. You need to come together and do this thing. Just do this thing!"

"But I did the best that I could. I'm so sorry. I did forget some things, but he was right there! I did the best I could . . ."

Cherri hugged me. Then Mike hugged me, too. I held him for a long time, and then we went out, the cameras following us.

The grand jury was held in April, with Claude Worrell back arguing for the Commonwealth. A few of Beebe's fraternity brothers who had been interviewed by police were called to testify, but that testimony is not part of the public record, and I was not present to hear it. Beebe appeared, but did not testify. The case was moved out of juvenile court to the circuit court, and Beebe was indicted on two felony counts: forcible rape and object sexual penetration: penetration of the victim by an animate (hand) or inanimate object.

Home again, we settled back into our lives. Once again, I reveled in the normalcy of motherhood and work. I went to PTA meetings, play dates, client meetings. I baked cupcakes with Ava. The investigation of my case continued, but at a less urgent pace. The trial seemed eons away. Still, I was in touch with Worrell and the police regularly, as more and more witnesses were unearthed.

Then, on November 9, 2006, Worrell e-mailed me: "Please call me when you have a minute." I picked up the phone immediately. My instincts told me this was not good news.

"Claude?"

Silence. And then, a sharp intake of breath.

"Liz, you were right. Beebe was one of three. Three men raped you that night and Beebe was the last. I am so sorry to be the one to tell you this."

I crawled under my desk and screamed at the top of my lungs.

CHAPTER 10

Dark Days and New Revelations

Worrell's revelation upended my already fragile sense of security. The legal process had empowered me in some ways, but was also a new source of stress. I had always darkly suspected I had been attacked by more than one person, with my foggy sense of a crowd and the rumors later, but hearing the confirmation was especially destructive to me. Having a gut feeling was very different than knowing there was evidence to support it. With this new information, my panic attacks increased in frequency and intensity. I tried deep breathing, yoga, giving up caffeine, creative visualization, grounding techniques, acupuncture, and meditation. Not even medication would help.

When I had first received the e-mails from Beebe, and way before I alerted the Charlottesville police in December 2005, I had sent notice to the University of Virginia's president, John Casteen, about the fact that a former student who had raped me was now in contact with me. I expressed concern that the University of Virginia Alumni Association had given Beebe my home address, despite the fact that he was not himself an alumnus, having never graduated from the university. I mentioned that I had met with the university police, Dean Sybil Todd by my side, on several occasions, and I requested any information he might be able to find in my file about the incident.

Casteen replied to say he had received my e-mail and would work diligently to get to the bottom of the problem. He copied his e-mail to others who might help me locate the file.

Later that day, a man named Leonard Sandridge, the chief operating officer of the university, informed me that he had communicated with the University of Virginia Police Department at the behest of President Casteen, and that, despite my many visits and reports made in the wake of the attack, "no record of the complaint can be found at this time." He also informed me that Student Health records were destroyed after ten years, so there was no paper trail of my visit to Student Health.

Months later, however, after the police were on the case, the chief of police, Tim Longo, referred in his press conference to a university report on my attack. This prompted a *Washington Post* reporter who was in touch with me to request the report, but the university rebuffed him. But after my testimony at the hearing I read a statement in an article from a university spokesperson saying that the report was legally mine to have. I wanted the *Post* reporter to be able to see it, so I wrote a formal request to the university's legal department to have the report sent to me.

One day, while Ava slept, I was sipping tea at my kitchen table when a large yellow envelope with a Charlottesville return address landed on my porch. It was thin. I slid the pages out and stared at them. My eyes scanned the five copied pages of handwriting. There was no letterhead, no date, no signature, and no official stamp. It was rife with black marks, redacted names, but my own name was front and center.

It stated that I had come to someone in authority to report an "alleged rape at Phi Kappa Psi house." People were interviewed. There were five interviewees in the report and, although the names were blacked out, one was clearly Jim Long, and another was Hud Millard. I had no idea who the others might be. They spoke of a party, of alcohol. One witness said he saw me lying bleeding on a sofa, but that he assumed I had been menstruating. Another witness claimed he saw me in a sheet lying on another floor bleeding, and then ran away. One witness tried to wake me up, but I only opened my eyes. One witness saw a man "running out of a room, with blood all over his pants" and "thought there had been a shooting," so he and his companion ran away to avoid any possible trouble. The report ended with the assertion that I had been advised by the university that I could speak with the Commonwealth's attorney but that I and my parents had turned down this option in the presence of Dean Canevari. It also stated that all options had been offered to me and my family and that I refused them and was referred to counseling. The pages dropped to the floor as I sat in shock, looking at this document of lies—the lies of scared student witnesses (or, now I thought, possible perpetrators?) and of the university, trying to make this incident look resolved. (Later, interviewed by Worrell at her home in Texas, Dean Todd said she had written this report, although her name was nowhere on it. Sadly, Dean Todd passed away from pancreatic cancer before the trial, and she defended the university's handling of the case to the end.) Since this document was the only official report from the time of the incident, the police and the attorneys clearly had a lot more work to do.

Worrell's new information came through Beebe's attorneys, and had been obtained by their team's private investigator. Their team offered the investigator's file to me in full for $30,000. It was a hefty price tag, and Mike and I were more than a little concerned that money could even buy such information; our own investigators were public servants, tied to bureaucratic purse strings. And who knew what was in the file? There was no guarantee that it was the kind of information we needed. I had to trust my own team to find the truth. Still, after the police had investigated all of the people I could remember from the party, the dorm, and the fraternity roster, they didn't have much to go on. Few people stepped forward to volunteer information, and many refused to cooperate with the police. Without a subpoena, no one can be forced to answer police questions. I'd like to think that if I ever had information about a crime, I would willingly share it. In this case, however, we were dealing with a tight-knit fraternity, and even all these years later, their bonds were ironclad. Besides, many were now prominent members of their communities and didn't want to touch this case. They maintained their silence.

After the bombshell about the gang rape, Worrell flew up to meet with me and prepare me for trial (scheduled for late November), a meeting we had planned even before this development. It was clear now that I had holes in my memory, which can be the kiss of death in the prosecution of a rapist, even one who has confessed. We would need to change our strategy as it related to my testimony.

When Worrell arrived, I was thrilled to see him and was burning with questions. We lunched at a restaurant two blocks from my home, taking a booth in the back, with both our notes spread on the table. He began to unravel the discoveries of the months since the preliminary hearing, based on the witness interviews.

The first was Hud Millard. Not surprisingly, I was very interested to hear his version of that night's events, although I was worried he would not remember them clearly, as he had been pretty drunk. Hud was now a pediatrician. He said he remembered working the door that night, remembered me and Jim arriving at the party. But he claimed to have left the party at eleven thirty P.M. and recalled nothing more. It was certainly curious. This was a man who was carried to a room, deposited there, and padlocked inside—presumably because the other brothers suspected he would intervene to help me. Perhaps he was embarrassed to admit that his brothers had done this to him. In any case, it appeared he had no interest in helping me now.

We had also wondered what had become of Beebe's roommate, Matt Westfall. Beebe had explained in his e-mail that what he did to me "he did upon Matt's bed" and that Westfall had been away for the weekend. Detectives Nick Rudman and Bob Sclafani had met with Westfall on a bench in New York's Central Park. He was disdainful toward them, and supportive of Beebe. He spoke of Beebe's "broken childhood." He didn't want to get involved, he said, as he was a "businessman of the utmost standing." Surely, Beebe would have had to explain to his room-mate what had happened. What had Beebe told him about the bloody sheets from his bed? What had Beebe told him about anything? Citing his "stellar business reputation," Westfall simply refused to cooperate.

Another especially compelling witness failed to cooperate. When I was shown a composite photograph of Phi Kappa Psi members, I identified Francis Woller as the individual who may very well have been the person who lifted me into Beebe's waiting arms. I also recalled that he had been in the second-floor party room and had actually been tending the bar for a while. As it turned out, Woller worked as a trader at a leading bank. Detective Rudman came to New York several times to interview him and was rebuffed each time, since Woller worked on a locked trading floor. Worrell and I discovered that Woller was the son of a much-loved elected government official. His father was a dear friend of President George W. Bush.

Worrell placed a call to Woller's father's office, admonishing him to tell his son to cooperate with authorities in the investigation. I was impressed with Worrell for standing up to this man. But for a long time, it had no effect. Woller went abroad on an extended work assignment of almost a year. However, when he returned, he hired himself a Charlottesville attorney and made some gestures of cooperation. He admitted to having purchased the strong grain alcohol that was in my green drink. He said he had been sent out to do so. He had nothing else to add.

John Block, the *Dateline* producer, who had been following the investigation and doing some detective work on his own, wanted to ask Woller further questions. He waited outside Woller's posh New York City apartment each day. Block told me that Woller, exasperated, allegedly said to a *Dateline* reporter, "What's in it for me to help this girl now?" His attorney sent a "cease and desist" letter to me in August 2008, disputing every word his client told police and threatening me with legal action should I disclose anything about his client.

There was another witness, Tuck Hammett, who had been missed by the Charlottesville police in the initial flurry of interviews. All these years later he was living alone on the outskirts of Charlottesville, in Albemarle County's quiet tranquillity. I did not know him, nor had I met him on the night in question. As it turned out, Hammett had been at a Grateful Dead concert with William Beebe the night I was raped, before coming back for the party. Hammett was no longer a student at that time. He had graduated, but remained a fraternity "adviser."

Detective Rudman and another officer caught up with him at his home in the country. Hammett was sitting on his porch, smoking a joint, when the car pulled up.

"Hey. I was wondering when you guys would find me!" he exclaimed.

The officers went inside and questioned him at great length. What they heard would be the basis for many other interviews and re-interviews of previously uncooperative subjects. Hammett spoke of "that girl the three guys had sex with" and described me and the three, believing it to be consensual. He told the story of how he had returned from the Grateful Dead show with Beebe and one other brother and how a girl was being "passed around" for sex. Hammett would be subpoenaed as a witness at the April grand jury. I don't know what he testified, but at that point only Beebe's actions were under scrutiny by the jury.

While the officers were at his house, Hammett mentioned that the RV parked on his lot belonged to one Nathan Burgos, a fraternity brother he remained good friends with. The name was familiar to the cops.

Nathan Burgos had been interviewed earlier in the investigation since he was listed in the yearbook as a Phi Kappa Psi brother, and the investigation had naturally started with any known members who were likely to have been at the house that night. Burgos, upon being interviewed by police, claimed to know nothing about the night in question, but other witnesses certainly remembered his being there. Burgos was older than most brothers owing to a tour in the United States Navy; according to various witnesses, he was known to "get girls drunk and take advantage of them." Burgos had allegedly been seen digitally raping me with four other men witnessing and cheering as he hiked my sweater above my neck and my skirt above my waist. It is alleged that this was the first attack, and it took place on the chapter-room floor while I was unconscious from the green drink. When the police came back to question Burgos after the press broke, he had left his wife and child and gone south. He claimed to have hired a lawyer. That lawyer had not been paid; he said he was not the attorney of record for Burgos. A grand jury subpoena was drawn up for Burgos, but he could not be found— he had become a veritable ghost. He never testified on the record.

I was sickened by this information. I had never heard Burgos's name, and when shown a photograph I could not recall his face. What he allegedly did to me was vile. But the story of what happened that night was about to get worse.

Another fraternity brother, Roger Messner, came under suspicion after a few of the brothers referred to me as "that girl Messner had sex with in his room."

Messner, like Burgos, had been questioned early in the investigation. A blueblood from Wilmington, Philadelphia, and Palm Beach, Messner had attended the prep school Choate, and had lived in the same dorm as William Beebe in their first year at UVA. He told police he had no idea who I was. In fact, he said, he was a virgin at the time of the alleged crime, and had remained so until the following year when he met his wife-to-be, so he couldn't possibly have raped me, or anyone else, for that matter.

But as the investigation progressed, witnesses began coming out of the woodwork regarding Messner's behavior that night. He had been seen dragging me to his bedroom on the third floor, one floor above Beebe's. The man who was Messner's roommate in the house testified that he had found me bleeding and unconscious in their room, after Messner walked to the showers, naked except for a towel, high-fiving friends along the way. How I then got to the second-floor chapter room and sustained the rape by Beebe remains a mystery. Were the injuries I sustained caused by Burgos or Messner or Beebe?

Armed with this new information, Detective Rudman drove to Messner's home in Wilmington, where he was living with his wife and children. When Rudman remarked, "Nice place you have here," Messner replied with a wistful sigh, "Well, it's all going to be gone in a year, isn't it?" The investigative team found this very telling. Messner stuck to his original story, but immediately hired a Charlottesville defense attorney, Timothy Heaphy, the son-in-law of General Eric Shinseki, the former United States Army four star general and current secretary of veteran affairs. Heaphy, a former United States attorney, had recently turned to criminal defense in Charlottesville with a focus on white-collar crime cases. (Heaphy was also attorney to Kirk Fordham, the former chief of staff of the disgraced Florida congressman Mark Foley.) Served a subpoena, Messner appeared before the grand jury. Reportedly, he took the fifth on every question, on the grounds of self-incrimination.

George Allman, the former fraternity president, now a professor at a Texas business school, was interviewed once on the phone by Detective Rudman. When Worrell and Quagliana went down to Austin to interview him, he had already retained counsel with the help of Phi Kappa Psi's national organization. He said he was not present in the house that weekend, and there was no reason to believe otherwise. Although he was one of the frat brothers who referred to me in interviews as "that girl Messner had sex with," he refused to say anything more regarding Burgos or Beebe. He did admit to calling Beebe's parents soon after, as Beebe was constantly drunk, using drugs, and threatening suicide. He cooperated no further in the investigation.

One witness, Bill Keller, came forward of his own accord once he heard about the case. A former lacrosse player, he was now an architect in Boulder, Colorado. He was incensed by the shame brought on the fraternity as a result of the rape. He remembered much of it and was willing to testify, refusing to let the bonds of brotherhood silence him.

Keller described to us a fraternity meeting mere days after the rape. The topic: the gang rape of a girl in the house—me. Other witnesses later corroborated this. A witness said William Beebe was present, curled up in a ball, sobbing, drunk, and possibly under the influence of drugs. George Allman, as he had said, called Beebe's parents to come collect him. Keller also described a brawl breaking out at the meeting; punches were thrown. It was clear that the brothers were divided over whether to co-operate with any police investigation of the incident or to try to keep it completely quiet. As it turned out, this was a moot point, since the police investigation never took place.

During this brawl, according to witnesses, David Hazzard, the son of a United States senator, stated that he was embarrassed that such a thing could occur at his fraternity house and that they were all acting like a bunch of animals. He demanded to know exactly what had happened. Apparently because his father was a senator, people told him. Hazzard, by all accounts, slapped Nathan Burgos clean across the face. But when Rudman and Sclafani questioned Hazzard, he insisted he had not been there and had no knowledge of the incident.

Once the scuffle was over, George Allman allegedly asked one of the brothers, Peter Melman, to call his father and arrange for personal insurance policies for each member of the fraternity "in the event that this should ever happen again." This story led my team to wonder if gang-raping a freshman was part of some rite of passage during rush at Phi Kappa Psi: a tradition of sorts.

Peter Melman was approached by police on a number of occasions at the gated community where he now lives in Annapolis, Maryland. When they rang the buzzer to his gate, he answered, "I don't have to speak with you and I don't have to let you in." He never obtained legal counsel of record. The cops spent days sitting outside of his complex, but he never surfaced. When they would ring his buzzer, he would simply repeat the fact that he did not have to speak with them. According to Worrell, it was Melman whose testimony could perhaps have provided the most information about what happened to me that night. Worrell wanted to get his hands on the purported insurance policies. If they had indeed been taken out, there was a clear action against the fraternity. Perhaps we shall never know. Melman, it was discovered, maintains steady friendships with Burgos, Hammett, and Messner.

Up to that point, Beebe had contended that I was in a healthy condition when the encounter between us occurred. Given the new theories about that night, this is hard to believe. Some witnesses suggested that Beebe, known to be socially awkward and unsuccessful with women, was goaded into "having a turn" after his late return from the Grateful Dead show with Tuck Hammett and another brother. One witness said Beebe dragged me screaming into his room, but that after raping me, while I was unconscious, he and a helper took me into the bathroom and tried to clean me up. After cleaning me up, they wrapped me in the sheet and deposited me on the sofa back in Beebe's room. Who helped him?

The evidence of witnesses who came into the room and saw me

bleeding, who saw Messner strut to the shower to wash my blood off, suggests that a cover-up plan must have been hatched. This begins to explain the empty house that Friday morning. Fraternity houses are known to be filled to capacity the mornings after a party, since no one goes to class, opting instead to sleep off the hangovers or continue to party into the morning hours. Our best guess is that everyone was instructed to get out of the house that night before I awoke—*if* I awoke—so that no one would be found culpable. Probably they hoped that I had ingested enough of the green drink to have no memory, or even die in what could have been called an accidental overdose or alcohol poisoning. What they didn't count on was that when I awoke, the extent of my injuries and amount of blood would be so evident and that I would remember my last attacker.

CHAPTER 11 *The Guilty Plea*

A week or so before the scheduled trial, Worrell called me to say that Beebe wanted to plead guilty to one count of felonious aggravated sexual battery, thereby taking the other counts of rape and object sexual penetration off the table. Well, of course he did. According to sentencing guidelines, if Beebe went to trial on the two felony charges, he was looking at a maximum sentence of life in prison. Although he was not likely to get the maximum sentence, it still made sense for him to cut a deal, and he was in a good negotiating position in light of the new information. The realities that made the crime worse for me—being raped by three men—made the situation a lot easier for him. Since I had no memory of the rapes by Burgos and Messner, my credibility would be called into question by the defense, yielding reasonable doubt that perhaps my memory of Beebe's crime was also unreliable.

Accepting the plea made sense for the Commonwealth, too. Even given Beebe's confession on record, the other two rapes made the case against him much weaker. Drawn-out trials quickly become expensive, and there was the possibility that if he went to trial, we might not get a conviction. There was also hope that as part of the plea bargain, the Commonwealth could get Beebe to testify against Messner and Burgos, strengthening the case against them, which for now was not strong enough for an indictment. We had some statements, but not enough corroboration. If Beebe cooperated, his testimony and the information from his private investigator could be very valuable.

Negotiations for a plea deal began. In a criminal case, these negotiations don't typically account for the victim's wishes; a state or commonwealth can cut a deal with a defendant regardless of what a victim or victim's family thinks. The victim is merely a witness, as I had been all along. Chapman and Worrell were kind enough to consult with me on my thoughts during the process. I am forever grateful that they brought me into the loop, although seeing just how this process worked was a bit of a shock.

First, Francis Lawrence came to Worrell and said that Beebe would agree to a plea of simple assault and serve six months. Worrell's response was, "Are we talking about the same crime?" he later told me. Simple assault is akin to punching someone. I had to say, I admired their chutzpah.

The next deal on the table was aggravated sexual battery, carrying a sentence of one and a half years. When Worrell brought this to me, I started to weep. At this point, the whole process had been going on for nearly two years. My child had been two years old when the letter arrived and she would be four on Christmas, a scant month away. With all the fear, stress, and renewed panic I had experienced, I felt as though I had already served a long sentence myself. Although it wasn't really up to me, and although the judge, regardless of the plea deal, can ultimately sentence the accused to any amount of time within the sentencing guidelines, I said I would feel better about a tougher sentence—maybe two years. Two years for aggravated sexual battery doesn't sound like much, given the severity of the crime, but there were many other balls in the air at this point—we could not lose our shot at having some agency in all of this madness. It seemed to me, Mike, and the team that given the new information, this was the best we could hope for, unless the judge decided otherwise. Two years it was. And in return, William Beebe would have to provide the prosecution with information about the other two men and the rapes that occurred that night.

We flew back down to Charlottesville on the morning of November 13, 2006, the day before the scheduled plea date, and checked into the same suite at the Boar's Head Inn where we had stayed when we went for our first interview with the Char- lottesville police. We ordered room service, went to the gym, tapped away on our BlackBerrys. I was calmer than I had been in weeks. We walked over to the court the next day with Worrell, who took us around the back. Crunching through the fall leaves reminded me of being a student here. This was my first time in circuit court, and it was a much bigger, grander courthouse than the juvenile court, where I had given my testimony. Presiding over the proceedings was Judge Edward Hogshire, a kindly older man. Hogshire took a look at the plea agreement, con- ferred with both prosecution and defense, and began.

NOVEMBER 14, 2006

THE COURT: All right, so we need to have Mr. Beebe stand for
arraignment.

Beebe stood up, dressed in a dark suit and white shirt, and I
was struck again by how very tall and large he was. He scared the
shit out of me, even in a public place.

CLERK: Are you William Nottingham Beebe?

WILLIAM BEEBE: I am.

CLERK: The grand jurors for the Circuit Court for the City of
Charlottesville in their April, 2006 term returned an
indictment charging on or about October 6, 1984, in
the City of Charlottesville, that you did, feloniously
and unlawfully, sexually abuse Elizabeth Seccuro nee
Schimpf, through her physical helplessness, in violation
of Virginia Code Section 18.2-67.3. How do you plead?

BEEBE: Guilty as charged.

You could feel the eyes of everyone in that courtroom turn to
me to see my reaction. I could hear a shift of people in their
benches, a rustling of papers. I began crying, burying my head on
Mike's tweed-clad shoulder.

Hogshire went on to ask Beebe some basic questions about his
date of birth, level of education, his understanding of the charges

against him. He was asked if he was taking this plea willingly and had been represented fairly by his attorneys. He was asked if he was pleading guilty of his own free will and if he was, indeed, guilty of the charges. He was informed that by pleading guilty, he would waive the right to appeal the court's decision. He was also informed that the crime he was pleading guilty to carried a maximum sentence of twenty years, regardless of the plea deal. It was standard stuff, but each answer seemed to bring us one step closer to a true end, after all this time.

THE COURT: All right, and, of course, it calls for you to plead guilty to the aggravated sexual battery indictment, and there is an agreed-upon sentence here, which is to be executed after the preparation of a pre-sentence report and that you and your attorneys have agreed on a maximum sentence of two years of active incarceration. Is that your understanding of the agreement?

BEEBE: It is.

THE COURT: The agreement also requires you to cooperate with the Commonwealth in this ongoing investigation as it relates to the other events which may have occurred on the date in question in this case. Do you understand that—October 6, 1984?

BEEBE: Yes, sir, I do.

THE COURT: It says, as long as you cooperate with that investigation in good faith and that the information provided to the Commonwealth is useful, the Commonwealth agrees to recommend a further reduction in your sentence, which will be at the discretion of the Commonwealth. Do you understand that?

BEEBE: Yes, sir.

THE COURT: All right, so I'm going to find that the plea was entered into freely and voluntarily and you have a seat with counsel. Mr. Worrell, if you will please summarize the Commonwealth's evidence in the case and the basis for the agreement.

At that point, Worrell briefly summarized the events of the night in question. It was hard to listen to, but I remained calm, focusing on the soothing qualities of Worrell's voice. But although I kept my focus on Worrell, I became aware that William Beebe was staring straight at me, intentionally and unabashedly. And I was not the only one who noticed—members of the media would later report on this, too, this unblinking stare. It was the most unsettling sensation I have ever experienced.

Worrell went on:

WORRELL: There is—and at the time of the preliminary hearing so the Court is aware, Ms. Schimpf's recollection of how that happened is different

from Mr. Beebe's recollection of how that
happened, in that Ms. Schimpf at the time of the
preliminary hearing testified that there was force
involved and Mr. Beebe said that there wasn't.
Part of the nature of this agreement is to
acknowledge that there are—well, divergent facts
about what happened and how it actually got to
where it did where Mr. Beebe confesses to and
admits to a sexual assault with Elizabeth Schimpf,
who was there in his room at that fraternity house.
And so that was really what drives the
Commonwealth to seek some resolution of the
matter, other than the charges that were initially
levied. What I can also say is that it also became
clear during the course of our investigation and
the Court became aware through other hearings
that we've had in this Court that the
Commonwealth believes that other sexual assaults
occurred that night, not by Mr. Beebe, but by
other individuals in that fraternity and that's what
we're continuing to investigate. And Mr. Beebe has
agreed to cooperate with the Commonwealth in as
far as he can in telling the Commonwealth what
he knows and what he recalls of these particular
events. And that too is particularly important to
the Commonwealth because we believe that the
matter doesn't end here, that there are other
things for the Commonwealth to do and other

individuals to pursue. Mr. Beebe's agreement to participate in our investigation and help us as best he can is important to the Commonwealth. But the major driving force, other than Mr. Beebe's participation, is the fact that in a jury trial, as the Court's well aware, you can almost never guarantee yourself a result. Here in this particular instance Mr. Beebe admits that he has committed a felony offense, he committed a felony sexual offense against Ms. Seccuro, then Schimpf, and has agreed to serve a penitentiary sentence, the precise length of which is unknown at the moment depending on what happens with the other cases.

THE COURT: All right, thank you, Mr. Worrell. Comments from the defense on the evidence on the plea agreement?

QUAGLIANA: Judge, the only thing—the only thing I would add on the issue of the sentencing guidelines is that Mr. Beebe appears before the Court this morning with no criminal record. He's been a law-abiding citizen for the 22 years since this occurred. We think that this plea to the aggravated sexual battery more closely approximates the facts of this case. Courts have difficulty accommodating the complexity of human situations and circumstances, but we think that this charge more

closely approximates what happened 22 years ago.
It acknowledges the role of alcohol, which I bring
up not to diminish Mr. Beebe's responsibility and
all that, but it is an important factor in the case.
Youth and other things that—that we think are
better encompassed by a plea to aggravated sexual
battery. So—thank you.

Blame youth. Blame alcohol. Blame the victim.

Judge Hogshire accepted the plea, and set March 15, 2007, as
a sentencing date. Beebe was free to go until that date, as long as
he complied with the terms of his bond. It was also agreed that
Beebe would be free to travel out of state until that date, which
was an unorthodox consideration for most accused felons awaiting sentencing. But from what I understood, Beebe had actually
been living in Florida while out on bond, helping to care for his
mother, who was very ill.

It saddened me to know that his mother was ill while her son
was facing these charges. I cannot imagine how difficult it must
have been for her to have her son taken from her, at this time
and under these circumstances. My own aging parents were also
having serious health issues. In the previous two years, my dad
had successfully battled throat cancer and was in remission. My
mom suffered from severe adult-onset hydrocephalus and was
confined to a wheelchair. They would be unable to come to the
sentencing, though they wanted to be at my side. I think, on
some level, they still wrongfully blamed themselves for letting
me go away to the University of Virginia at all. Listening to the

proceedings, seeing Beebe in the flesh, might have been too much for them to bear.

Back outside the courthouse, Mike and I made brief statements to the media about the plea and what that meant in terms of justice. We tried to be upbeat. We said we were pleased with the arrangement, and looked forward to getting back to our daughter and our lives. Furthermore, the outcome gave survivors a real story to believe in. There can be vindication; there can be some sense of justice. Because I spoke out in 1984, and because years later I didn't just accept an apology, this was a victory for all survivors, not just for me. We thanked everyone who had helped us on the long road. Beebe also made a statement on the steps of the courthouse, talking about how he hoped his pleading to a lesser offense would bring some sense of closure to me and my family. It was the first time he spoke publicly about the case.

Mike and I returned home, spent. But there was more to come—the larger investigation was gaining steam. There was some hope that another grand jury would be called. Although it was doubtful that either of the other two suspects would ever come forward and confess, the police did have new information provided by Beebe's investigator, and they were re-interviewing all of the witnesses.

When I had first heard of Messner's comment about the possible loss of his home, I had jumped up and down. Wasn't that sort of an admission of guilt? Or was it merely a statement that he would have to spend enormous resources defending himself? Messner had refused to answer questions at the original grand jury. Now, he said nothing more. He kept the same

Charlottesville-based attorney and stuck to his story that he had never met me; he had been a virgin until the day he married his wife. This latter part I find laughable—and yet, if taken as a half truth, it could actually explain how he might have gotten involved in the crime. Virgin second years were hard to find in fraternities, and it would not have surprised me if someone had challenged his manhood, spurring him to the deeds he allegedly committed against me that night. My thoughts and heart went out to his wife and children, something I did not have to consider with Beebe. They had done nothing and I could not bear the thought of these poor family members ostracized in the community because of something terrible their father and husband would not confess to or even testify about.

Meanwhile, Burgos was in an undisclosed location. His RV remained parked on the grounds of Tuck Hammett's home in the Charlottesville area, and although we all felt that Hammett had more to say, he receded into the background of the investigation.

The web became more and more entangled as my anxiety level kept creeping up. As time passed, it became clear that another grand jury would not be convened. Beebe had not been as helpful as we had hoped, and we couldn't get any more out of him. From a financial perspective, with my legal team limited by the city budget, it didn't seem to make sense to convene a grand jury without the hard evidence that would guarantee further criminal indictments. We all knew there was much more to the story, but perhaps we would have to be satisfied with only one assailant being charged and eventually serving some time. The system is not perfect, but it is what we have, and I did not want to spend the rest of my life chasing down the broken pieces of the puzzle. Although I wanted and deserved the truth, and wanted justice served, in some ways perhaps I was better off not knowing everything that had transpired that night. In the end, I felt grateful that I didn't remember every heartbreaking detail.

Celebrating the Christmas holiday that year, I was far more engaged in life. I found myself thinking less and less about the case and more about the fact that I should be proud to have opened my mouth and said something. With all of the sensationalism swirling about, it came down to one fact: I stood up for what was right. As the mother of a little girl, that was the best gift I could ever have given her.

CHAPTER 12 *The Sentencing of William Beebe*

The sentencing of a criminal is certainly the end of a long journey for victims, but it can also be a painful last step as the defense team jockeys for the lightest possible sentence for their client, regardless of the agreed-upon plea deal. A judge can overturn that deal if he or she finds cause, and the defense attorney's main goal is to minimize his or her client's exposure to prison. Character witnesses are brought forth to trumpet the defendant's good qualities and point to all of the admirable things the perpetrator has done. Beebe's sentencing was to be no different. Quagliana wanted to submit videotapes of Beebe's ill mother, and scores of letters from Beebe's friends and parade a veritable who's who of the Richmond AA community before the court on March 15. But this would also be my chance to talk about the lasting impact his assault had had on me—the impact that couldn't be erased by apologies or later good deeds. We were talking about the night in question. My victim impact statement, which I had been required to submit to the court ten days prior to sentencing, was the document in which I got to tell my story in my own words, not twisted by cross-examinations. I would be allowed to read my statement to the court and be heard.

MARCH 15, 2007

THE COURT: Okay, this is Commonwealth versus William
Beebe. We're here for sentencing. I've been
delivered a set of guidelines with a pre-sentence
report. Mr. Worrell, is the Commonwealth going
to be offering those at this time?

THE COURT: I've only seen the one, so—which has the
offender's version in it, so can we go ahead and
admit those at this point?

RHONDA QUAGLIANA: Yes, Your Honor, thank you.

THE COURT: All right.

CLAUDE WORRELL: There's also—the Court has received the
victim impact statement and we'd ask
the Court to receive that also.

THE COURT: All right, let's see. When was the victim impact
statement?

WORRELL: You should have received that maybe three or four
days ago, Judge.

THE COURT: Yeah, I don't see that. It may be in the file
somewhere.

I gasped as I realized that the document I had worked on for
a month, attempting to be as balanced and clear as possible, to
make the court and Beebe understand what the impact had

been on my family, had not even been reviewed by Judge Hogshire.

WORRELL: Judge, it's pretty long and it's pretty detailed. You might want to take ten—fifteen minutes to read it. It's not short.

THE COURT: Why don't we get started and then—and then, if I need to take some time, I'll—I'll be sure I've covered it, but why don't we get the hearing started and I'll be sure I'll—I would have finished this before we conclude the case and I may take a recess in order to do that—

WORRELL: Okay.

I could tell Worrell shared my frustration as it had been his job to make certain I submitted the statement in the time allowed for proper review.

A man named Jeffrey Lenert was called to testify. He was a probation officer for the Virginia Department of Corrections, and he had prepared the pre-sentencing report on Beebe. Worrell asked whether Beebe had complied with his reporting requirements thus far and asked where he would live upon release. Lenert admitted that he did not know—the rules for reporting and even Beebe's length of sentence seemed to differ, depending on whom he spoke to within the department. When he called the secretary of the Virginia Parole Board—a separate entity—she had estimated that Beebe could be released in six months. This testimony caused much rumbling in the courtroom, but Lenert wasn't finished. The parole board secretary had later called him back: she had been mistaken, and he would have to direct his inquiry to another person in his own department. But that other person was unable to give any sort of estimate regarding the length of Beebe's incarceration. Although Lenert kept phoning to get an answer, no one returned his call, and thus there was no information about the true length of Beebe's sentence currently available for him to submit to the court.

This all sounded like a bureaucratic nightmare, and left both the gallery and the judge thoroughly confused.

After a few more questions from both Quagliana and Worrell—confirming, for example, that Beebe would have to register in Virginia as a sex offender—the judge determined that very little could really be learned regarding probation or parole, and moved on. He also promised to take a recess shortly to review my victim impact statement.

For now, Quagliana took the floor.

QUAGLIANA: If I may, the Commonwealth has agreed that I may proffer certain information for the Court's consideration at sentencing. To begin with, I would proffer that Mr. Beebe has been cooperative with authorities. Detective Rudman is in the courtroom. Detective Rudman would tell the Court that Mr. Beebe voluntarily gave a statement to him and was cooperative with him. Following an interview that Detective Rudman

did with Mr. Beebe, Mr. Beebe was arrested in
Las Vegas. He was arrested on January 4th of
2006, and he was held in the Clark County Jail for
six days. He was released by a Nevada judge. The
condition of his release in Nevada was that he
returns to that Court. There was no condition
placed upon him that he come to Virginia;
nonetheless, he came to Virginia voluntarily. He
got on a plane and came here on the 15th to face
his charges. On the 17th, he turned himself in and
he was released on bond. He has had meetings
with Mr. Worrell and Detective Rudman and
another detective from the Charlottesville Police
Department. He shared information with them.

THE COURT: Do you want to go ahead and—you have some
witnesses you want to put on?

QUAGLIANA: I do, Your Honor.

Quagliana called the first character witness, a young woman
named Marcie. She told the court that she had known Beebe since
1994, when she was thirteen years old and an addict. At that time
in her life, she bathed once every three months, shampooed her
hair only twice a year, and had embezzled $24,000 from one of
her employers. When she found sobriety and William Beebe in
Alcoholics Anonymous, she turned her life around. He would
help her get to meetings, take her to the Laundromat, and basically make sure her life was on the straight and narrow. She stated

that he had never told her about what he had done at the University of Virginia. She herself had never been prosecuted for the embezzlement. Instead, at Beebe's suggestion, she tried to make amends by anonymously donating $24,000 to a charity.

The next witness called was an older woman named Kristi, who had lived in Richmond for fifty years and worked at Offender Restoration. In her job she visited prisons and helped inmates who struggled with addiction and sobriety. She had met Beebe in 1994, when he began volunteering at Pamunkey Regional Jail. She said he was very active in helping prisoners transition to a life of sobriety. When asked, she also said Beebe had never mentioned the incident at the University of Virginia in 1984.

A gentleman named William G. was next. He was a full-time stay-at-home father in Richmond who had met Beebe at an AA meeting eleven years before. He had struggled with sobriety, and credited Beebe with saving his life. He also testified that when his child developed a life-threatening disease, Beebe took classes on how to help care for the child's medical needs, learning CPR and how to intubate the child. But he also allowed that Beebe's current sobriety did not excuse his past behavior.

All of these character witnesses made a powerful impression. They sat together on the side of the defense, occasionally smiling and nodding at Beebe, who sat at the defense table. Clearly, he had a tight-knit community in recovery.

Finally, Quagliana called Alex Downing, the man with whom Beebe had been living since leaving custody in Charlottesville in January 2006. He seemed to be the person closest to Beebe, and Mike and I were very curious to hear his testimony.

DIRECT EXAMINATION BY RHONDA QUAGLIANA

QUAGLIANA: Mr. Downing, will you tell the Court your full name, please?

ALEX DOWNING: My full name is Joseph Frederick Alexander Downing, III.

QUAGLIANA: Where do you live?

DOWNING: I live in Richmond, Virginia.

QUAGLIANA: Okay. Are you married?

DOWNING: Yes.

QUAGLIANA: What's your wife's name?

DOWNING: Valerie.

QUAGLIANA: Do you have any children?

DOWNING: I have a step-son who's sixteen.

QUAGLIANA: How are you employed?

DOWNING: I'm employed by a publisher.

QUAGLIANA: How long have you been employed by them?

DOWNING: A little over fourteen years.

QUAGLIANA: Okay. Do you know Mr. Beebe?

DOWNING: I do.

QUAGLIANA: Okay, and how do you know him?

DOWNING: Originally, when we met he was friends with my wife for it could have been a year or two before I met him, perhaps, probably shorter than that— through my wife.

QUAGLIANA: Okay, and has he been staying with you while he's been released on bond?

DOWNING: Yes, ma'am. Other—

QUAGLIANA: At your home in Richmond?

DOWNING: Yes, ma'am.

QUAGLIANA: Okay. What kind of person is he?

DOWNING: I know Will to be very caring, very trustworthy, interested in others. He likes animals. I've got eight cats, so that's important to me.

QUAGLIANA: Okay, and that's including over a period of time when—let's say, you've had a full house. You have somebody who is not a member of your family living with you for a little over a year, correct?

DOWNING: Correct.

QUAGLIANA: Okay. Has he provided help and support to you and your wife in the past?

DOWNING: Yes, I mean, it—we do that a lot for each other. That could be from I have to drop my car off because it's getting worked on to I need a ride to somewhere across town to, you know, my wife had to leave. Her grandfather is pretty much on his death bed in Texas and she couldn't be here today and I didn't have cash for a cab at four A.M. to get to the airport and, I mean, it's just whatever I needed, Will was there.

QUAGLIANA: Okay. How would you describe the level of Mr. Beebe's commitment to staying sober?

DOWNING: If there's a percentage higher than a hundred, that's what I would call it, and I know that he knows, like I do, that that's what has to be done in order to stay there.

QUAGLIANA: Okay. Have you ever observed him do or say anything that caused you to question in any way his commitment to his sobriety?

DOWNING: Absolutely not.

QUAGLIANA: Okay. Is it just the opposite?

DOWNING: Yes.

QUAGLIANA: Okay. While he was in your home over the past, I guess it's been about fourteen months, is that— does that sound right?

DOWNING: I think it was close to a year before he was allowed— almost a whole year before he was allowed to go to take care of his mother in Florida.

QUAGLIANA: Okay. Did he abide by all of the conditions of his bond?

DOWNING: Absolutely.

QUAGLIANA: Okay, and let me pull you back just for a second. How important is Will's help to other people in maintaining his own sobriety and his outlook on life?

DOWNING: It's absolutely critical. There is no other way to describe it.

QUAGLIANA: Thank you. Those are my questions.

THE COURT: Questions, Mr. Worrell?

WORRELL: Yes, sir.

CROSS-EXAMINATION BY CLAUDE WORRELL

CLAUDE WORRELL: Mr. Downing, Mr. Beebe lived with you up until the time he went to Florida, is that right?

DOWNING: Yes, sir.

WORRELL: Had he lived with you previous to that?

DOWNING: No.

WORRELL: You would describe yourself as being Mr. Beebe's friend, is that right?

DOWNING: Correct.

WORRELL: You've been friends for how long?

DOWNING: I would say approximately twelve years. I don't remember the actual first meeting, but it would be a good ballpark.

WORRELL: During that twelve-year time period, Mr. Beebe had been sober, is that right?

DOWNING: Correct.

WORRELL: You said you met him through your wife?

DOWNING: Yes, sir.

WORRELL: In the course of your wife's meeting Mr. Beebe— well, let me ask you this. How did she meet Mr. Beebe?

DOWNING: To be honest with you, I'm not sure. Probably from a fellowship group to which we all belong.

WORRELL: Is that a church fellowship or some other kind of fellowship?

DOWNING: No, sir, it's a spiritual fellowship.

It was weird that none of these witnesses wanted to call Alcoholics Anonymous by its name. Claude's impatience showed.

WORRELL: What's that?

DOWNING: We practice spiritual principles and try to serve others. I mean, can you be more specific?

WORRELL: Well, can you be more specific? What kind of group is this?

DOWNING: I can.

WORRELL: Is it called anything? Is it—

DOWNING: It is. It's called Alcoholics Anonymous.

WORRELL: Okay, and in that group, are you also a participant in that group?

DOWNING: Yes, sir.

WORRELL: AA has as a part of its core some principles and steps that one must get into and deal with in order to be or successfully go through the program, I suppose. It's got steps involved, is that right?

DOWNING: Yes, sir.

WORRELL: Is there also something called The Big Book that's also involved in the AA program?

DOWNING: Yes. It makes—it makes—it calls them suggestions. It has an outline.

WORRELL: Is it up to you, then, to follow the suggestions to the best of your ability, or do you believe that it's up to you to actually follow what the Book says and the suggestions literally?

DOWNING: I believe what the Book says applies to me. I can't speak for any other person other than myself when it comes to that. I've found that it has changed my life.

WORRELL: You would also—and would you also say that the Book is, from what you can see at least, has done the same for Beebe—Mr. Beebe?

DOWNING: Yes, sir.

WORRELL: All right, and his adherence to the principles outlined in the book, would you say he's a literalist?

QUAGLIANA: Judge, I'm going to object. I think we're getting into speculation by this witness.

THE COURT: Well, I don't know where—is this taking us somewhere? I don't know where—

WORRELL: Well, absolutely.

THE COURT: Okay.

WORRELL: Mr.—Mr. Downing has told us how great Mr. Beebe is and how great he did this thing and how wonderful he is about this and wonderful he is about that, and—okay, but is there also some other things that Mr. Downing might be able to tell us about with Mr. Beebe because as what we have as part of this case, as the Court is aware, that Mr. Beebe was in an AA group and made amends as required by one of the steps in that book, and the question is, is he a literalist about that? [A]nd that's part of this case. Mr. Downing knows the book. He also knows Mr. Beebe and he can tell us the answer.

DOWNING: I would not classify Will as a literalist. I would say that he looks probably similarly as I do as that this is the outline for living. A literalist to me, as the question is asked, means that there is no room for anything different than other than exactly what the word says on the page. I don't try to put my own words in there at all. That's a little bit dangerous, but you can get different opinions on the same sentence.

WORRELL: What is step nine?

DOWNING: Make direct amends to such people wherever possible, except when to do so would injure them or others.

WORRELL: Is that what the book actually says or is that something else that's said in the book? Are those the exact words—what you just repeated?

DOWNING: I believe that those are the exact words. When I say I believe, I—you—I may have missed an and or something, but I think that's pretty close.

WORRELL: It's probably pretty fair to say that you know that book pretty well.

DOWNING: I try to practice it. I would say that would be a fair statement.

WORRELL: Does the book tell you anything about what to do if harm does come to another person?

DOWNING: You—in what context, sir?

WORRELL: Well, what does step nine say?

DOWNING: Make direct amends to such people wherever possible, except when to do so would injure them or others.

WORRELL: Okay, and so what happens when you injure another person by acting on step nine? Does the book give you any guidance there?

To me, this had developed into the core of the case. I had been criticized by many people for pressing charges when Beebe was "just trying to apologize." But what happens when your amends cause further harm?

DOWNING: Not explicitly. The only thing that—that I can— there's a part earlier where it talks about nine times out of ten the unexpected happens, which is— means that things essentially go fairly well, and there's another part right next to that that talks about that—the example they use is getting thrown out of someone's office, and if we've attempted to make the amend and they've, sort of, rejected us, then that's—we've done the best that we can with that. It doesn't speak specifically, that I'm aware of, and you, by all means, might be able to correct me. I don't have it all memorized, that, you know, if I injured someone trying to make amends to them, you know, it's almost like I would just be running in a circle.

WORRELL: Right, but whatever it is, you have to be able to stand ready to do whatever that person would like you to do.

DOWNING: I would say that that's mostly true. If I—if I treated someone shabbily that I had dated, for example, not anything in a illegal sense, but if I just, you know, belittled them in public or something and I went back to do that and they said, well, it will be okay with me if you pay me five thousand dollars ($5,000), that—I'm using an outrageous example just to make a point. It's not here's, you know, an open check no matter what. What if they ask me to break the law? I don't—it's kind of hard to totally answer that question.

Downing stepped off the stand. Quagliana then asked another ten or so members of the gallery to stand, identify themselves, and tell the court how long they had known Mr. Beebe. All were members of his AA group. The judge decided not swear each one in and have more of the same testimony, but they stood to show their support. Next, Quagliana offered a sheaf of letters from Beebe's AA friends in Las Vegas—more of the same. The judge accepted them, agreeing to review them at the recess along with my statement.

While this outpouring of fellowship was impressive, it hit me that all of these witnesses were from the AA community. Their stories were identical. Beebe had clearly made AA his life, but there was no one here who knew Beebe at the time he raped me, nor even in the decade after. No fraternity brothers. No family members. Quagliana seemed desperate to convince us that this Beebe was a whole new person, that the criminal of the past had disappeared. This reminded me, in a way, of what I'd heard from the university, so many years ago. *The person who did this to you is gone; why won't you give this up?*

During the recess, Mike, Worrell, and I conferred in the back vestibule of the courtroom. Worrell had some devastating news. I would not be able to read my victim impact statement in open court. Mike was not allowed to make a statement on our behalf, either. I was gutted, gob-smacked. Victim impact was my one chance to say "I forgive you" or "You ruined my life" or simply "This was the fallout," and to do so in court, in front of those attorneys, those character witnesses, my friends, the media, and, most important, Beebe. The core of sentencing is not only to hear the good things the defendant has done with his life, but to hear the impact the crime has had on the victim and his or her family. Hearing both sides is the heart and soul of the justice system. I could not understand why I was being silenced once again. All victims and secondary victims of crime are granted the right to read an impact statement in court at sentencing. Why was my situation any different? Worrell explained that because the case had become more complicated with the revelation of the multiple assailants, and because the investigation remained open, Quagliana would actually be allowed to cross-examine me or Mike on anything we said in our victim impact statements. It would have widened the scope of the proceedings and I would have effectively been put on trial myself. It is worth mentioning that not all jurisdictions would allow this cross-examination, but in the case of *Commonwealth of Virginia v. Beebe*, it would be allowed, as unorthodox as it seemed. Given the holes in my memory, this could be a liability for the prosecution—not to mention a huge challenge for me emotionally. It wasn't a risk Worrell could take. I accepted this, but couldn't hold back my frustration.

We returned to the courtroom and the judge again took the bench. The next issue was the extent to which Beebe had cooperated with the ongoing investigation—a condition of the plea agreement. This was another source of frustration for me. We had cut the deal so that Beebe might open up and give us more information for the investigation. And while he had, in the strictest sense, cooperated, meeting with Worrell and Detective Rudman on two occasions, he hadn't provided anything of actual value. It didn't seem right to me that the deal was still on the table. But what was done was done. We moved to final summations.

In Worrell's summation, though he couldn't make up for my own unread statement, he tried to make clear the impact of the crime on my life and that of my family. He recommended that the judge impose a full two-year sentence. He pointed out, too, the impact of the apology letter, which had caused a new round of pain. He insisted that if the letter had been sent in good faith, Beebe should have been prepared to face the consequences of his serious crime.

Quagliana stood up for her rebuttal. Her last chance to minimize Beebe's sentence. As expected, she had a different view of Beebe's letter: "What he did in writing the letter was to leave the rest up to her. In turn, she chose to begin an e-mail conversation with Mr. Beebe." She described how the correspondence revealed different "scripts" of the crime for me and Beebe:

QUAGLIANA: Ms. Seccuro describes a violent attack.

Mr. Beebe describes a nineteen year old, sort of, hapless guy who's drunk himself, who sees a woman or a girl who he thinks he can have sex with and he acts on that impulse, and he knows it's wrong because he knows that under other circumstances this young lady wouldn't have stayed with him, wouldn't have had sex with him and—and that's wrong and he knows that and it bothers him for the next twenty-two years. Just like, you know, we've all done things in our life.

She focused on his cooperation (such as it was) with the authorities. She asked for leniency.

Worrell was allowed a rebuttal.

WORRELL: There is one more thing I'd like to leave the Court with and I'd like you to consider this for a moment. When the defendant was—or Ms. Quagliana, for defendant, was summarizing, she said Mr. Beebe sent her a letter and the choice was up to her. The choice was up to her. What choice is that? The only thing that Elizabeth Seccuro has had choice about as it relates to Mr. Beebe is whether or not to call the Charlottesville Police Department after she received this letter in September of 2005 . . . But as it relates to Mr. Beebe, Elizabeth Seccuro has never had a choice, and that is certainly the point of every sexual assault case that we have, every sexual assault law that we have. It's really about overbearing someone's will and imposing your choices upon them, and there can't really be any more significant way of doing that than the way in which Mr. Beebe did that when, at the time, Ms. Seccuro couldn't say no because she was, in the eyes of the law, helpless, and it seems to the Commonwealth that when you take advantage of helpless people, we're not talking about a sentence that is lenient or a term of months.

I can tell you now that Elizabeth Seccuro would
certainly be pleased with a two-year penitentiary
sentence. That's what she wants, that's her choice,
and isn't it about time that the criminal justice
system and we-all that are involved in it try to do
something that approximates that for her?—because
that is really the measure of what justice is
here.

At last, Beebe was allowed to speak on his own behalf. Yet
another choice I didn't have.

THE COURT: All right. Mr. Beebe, is there anything you'd like
    to tell the Court before I impose sentence, sir?

WILLIAM BEEBE: Yes, I do, Your Honor[.] My only purpose in
    contacting Ms. Seccuro was to make
    amends for my conduct twenty-two years
    ago. I am not trying to excuse my behavior,
    but I was a different person then. I was an
    immature nineteen year old with a drinking
    problem I did not yet fully understand. Even
    then, however, I understood that I didn't
    treat Ms. Seccuro with respect. As a person
    who injured or harmed another seeks
    atonement for his transgression, when I
    wrote the letter, I recognized it would be up

to Ms. Seccuro to a large extent when she thought that I had achieved enough atonement for my wrong. In contacting her a year-and-a-half ago, I was trying to do the best I could, both broadly and specifically to employ principles which have worked well in the past with others, regardless of the offense, and this idea as my lawyer pointed out was contained in the letter—the original letter that I wrote her in which I invited dialogue on her time and on her terms. I did my best to meet Ms. Seccuro on the emotional level. I did my best to set things right and to demonstrate a willingness to accept whatever thoughts and feelings she had been experiencing. In contacting her, I never intended to cause hurt or harm to her. I've never tried to contact her directly in person, to go to her home, or to otherwise invade her personal space. In our communication, I have respected her wishes and I will always continue to do that. Twenty-two years ago I was not mature enough to accept and live by effective guiding principles for making amends to those I had harmed in some fashion. Then, there was no solution that I could or would see. It was not until thirteen years ago when

I became willing to address all my mistakes in accountability using these tenants [*sic*] that I could even stay sober, let alone find the inner freedom that I have today. Since that time, in adopting a new way of life, I have a purpose and that gives life meaning. I didn't have that then. I believe that more lessons will be revealed from all of this, not just for me, but for the many because it's garnered so much attention. I believe that I've done everything I can to this point to right the wrong twenty-two years ago. Thank you for hearing me.

THE COURT: Any reason I shouldn't impose sentence today?

BEEBE: No, sir.

It was time for the sentence.

THE COURT: All right. Well, this case is unique in many ways; unfortunately, the circumstances of the case are not unique for those of us who live in and practice law for years in a college town. And I think it's an interesting case from the point of view of, one, it's clearly not a minor assault. It's not a minor thing. It is a horrific thing that this woman has been through, and it's, clearly, from her impact statement, it has had a profound

231

effect on her life without question, so, there are deep emotional wounds here that only time and counseling and good friends can help ameliorate. On the other side is that we look at someone like Mr. Beebe, whose life starting, I think in the early mid-nineties[,] has been one who's been a leader in the recovery community in ways that I, very frankly, have never seen before. I think there needs to be a felony sanction, and I'm going to tell you what I think the fair sanction is. I think there should be a ten-year penitentiary sentence, but with all but one year and six months suspended and I know it's parole eligible, and I'm saying that because I really feel like he is no—there's no indication he hasn't cooperated, and I think there ought to be some good faith benefit to this. At the same time, I think the suspension ought to be conditioned on his performing substantial community service and no one has mentioned that, but I think Mr. Beebe is in a unique position to help address what is—I see as almost a rampant issue of alcohol abuse on our college campuses. What we know here is that it's not consensual, and this was not something that a young woman has agreed to do and her life is terribly altered as a result of what's happened, so I think there has to be a consequence for that, and so what I'm going to recommend is that there be community service—five hundred hours of community service devoted to addressing the issues of sexual assault and alcohol abuse on college campuses if we can do that. I would prefer it be directed at UVA just because that's my alma mater. That's my—that's my homeland, but it can be anywhere. I think there should be ten years of good behavior, two years of general supervision, obviously, no alcohol, and I'd like to see the community service completed within the period of supervised probation and court costs will need to be paid during the first year of supervised probation. Any other issue that needs to be addressed that we haven't covered?

WORRELL: I just ask the defendant's bond be revoked and he be taken into custody now.

THE COURT: All right.

WORRELL: Is he ready to go ahead and be remanded today?

QUAGLIANA: Your Honor, I think our expectation was that if the Court imposed—

THE COURT: An active sentence, he'd go ahead and be remanded today?

QUAGLIANA: Thank you, Your Honor.

WORRELL: One more thing I'd ask.

THE COURT: Yes.

WORRELL: No contact, please.

THE COURT: No contact with the victim or her family, yeah, and I thought that would be a request and—all right. All right, folks, so we'll—anything else? Does that do it?

WORRELL: Yes.

THE COURT: All right, we covered it all? All right, good luck to you, Mr. Beebe. Good luck to you, Ms. Seccuro. All right.

The gavel slammed down and it was over. Out of the corner of my eye, I saw William Beebe steal a glimpse at me and I turned abruptly toward my husband for safety. My back to the defense table, I missed the moment, but I heard it. The click of the metal handcuffs around his wrists. No one can describe that lonely feeling—it's not a happy day for rape victims to have their perpetrator go to prison. As victims, we are never really free. We understand what freedom is. To be partially responsible for someone else's losing his freedom did not feel good. But I felt it was right, was just, was warranted. That cold *click* sent a shudder through me as I realized there was an end to this part of the story and a new dawn on the horizon.

Mike and I stepped from our bench and walked up the aisle toward the front entrance. I avoided coming face-to-face with Beebe. I didn't see him being loaded into the waiting van that was to whisk him to the local prison. As we stepped into the foyer, we were met by the media. I had hoped to make my statement in court, to the parties involved in the case. But I was left making a statement to the media. I removed my sunglasses, revealing eyes that were rimmed with red from crying. I started crying again as I read my statement. I thanked everyone who had worked on my behalf and supported me, and I talked about healing and hope. The whirr of the shutters clicking and the boom mikes just above my head were immensely disorienting. I stumbled through my statement, at one point handing it over to Mike so that he could read it in my place. There were a few questions. Then we got in our car. We were going home.

The sentence felt light to me, but I understood it was the law. Two years was what I had expected after our discussions with Worrell. I could understand the judge's sympathy toward Beebe, based on the testimony regarding his life in the past decade or so. It was clear that Hogshire did not believe Beebe to be a continued threat. I could not be sure; I really knew very little about Beebe's life, either before or after the attack. But I knew for sure that he had committed a violent crime, and I felt that, for now, prison was where he should be. Furthermore, I felt uneasy at the notion of Beebe's doing community service on college campuses and, specifically, the University of Virginia, the scene of the crime and the site of an investigation that was still ongoing. I understood the judge's impulse: community service in general is not a bad idea, and I think the judge believed that Beebe's sharing his story on campuses might prevent similar crimes. But there was a certain "fox in the hen house" feeling to sending him back to the University of Virginia. Besides, as I had begun to speak on campuses around the country myself, and seen how students responded to me, I felt that my story, my message, was the one they needed to hear. Not just "Rape could land you in jail," but "Rape is a horrific crime, with a lifelong impact on the survivor." My message was also about students' protecting themselves and others—not something I felt Beebe was qualified to address. It didn't feel right.

I buried myself in my work once again. There was a profound happiness in my renewed productivity, and in doing good work for my clients. I resumed therapy. It was a different "normal," but it was my normal nonetheless. Mike was considering asking for his old job back. Ava was joyous and had begun kindergarten around Labor Day. Life was good.

One day in mid-September 2007, I was sitting in my office when the phone rang. I answered in my usual lilt, "Hello, Dolce Parties!" I heard a click and a hollow sound. I almost hung up—yet another telemarketer. But I paused. And a tinny, canned, prerecorded voice informed me that my "offender would be released from the Charlottesville-Albemarle jail on September 14." I slammed the phone down in a panic. Certainly, this couldn't be true. Some error in the automated victim notification system. He had just gone to prison! I began dialing furiously:

my husband, Chief Longo, Claude Worrell, Jeffrey Lenert in probation. Lenert was the one who picked up. Yes, it was true. I asked how that could possibly be, but he said he did not know. It was simply "computed" that way.

Worrell called me back. He hadn't heard the news, but promised to get more information. Chief Longo called next—he hadn't heard anything, either. No one at corrections could confirm why or when. Finally, Worrell called again. There had been a "computer error." William Beebe's data had not been entered into the system properly. He had not been classified as a violent offender, and thus was still sitting in the regional jail, not one of the maximum security facilities we had expected. Due to this lack of classification, his lack of a prior criminal record, his good behavior, and the fact that the regional jail was at 150 percent capacity, Beebe was being released. Just like that, a two-year recommendation for a felony sentence had boiled down to five months and change.

But there was nothing we could do now. Beebe had served his sentence, regardless of the administrative issues surrounding his release. He was released on September 14, just as the automated call had warned. News crews showed photographs of a long-haired, goateed man who looked nothing like the defendant in the courtroom over five months ago. As Beebe regained his freedom, I again lost a sense of mine. This didn't feel like justice, but this was the result of our system—a good system, if flawed. I saw no reason to continue to fight this. I didn't want to spend the rest of my life mired in thoughts of William Beebe. At this point, only I could make this feel right, and I wanted something good to come of it. I focused on how I could make a difference for other survivors.

And with that resolve, my life began anew.

Hope, Joy, and the Continuing Fight

W hat does it sound like when your planet crashes wide open? For me, it was the skittery, papery *pffft* of an envelope sliding across my lap as I sat in the passenger seat of my car in my driveway. It was a letter. It was Thursday, September 5, 2005, when my past came skidding into my present, and at that precise moment, I realized that my day-to-day existence would change. I knew instinctively, with certainty, what that envelope contained, and yet I opened it. I was curious. Curious to know why, who, what, when? And although my life did change, at the end of the day I still don't think I have the answers. What happened to me that night in 1984 is ultimately unknowable, no matter how many people raise their right hands and swear to tell the Truth, the whole Truth, and nothing but the Truth. But I have come to believe that living with *that*—the unknowable— is the brave part.

What I am able to know, I am able to forgive. To a large extent, I think my case got so much attention not because of concern about rape, or campus crime—there are, unfortunately, so many crimes like it—but because of the issue of forgiveness. Commentators seemed to think that because Beebe had apologized, I should have forgiven, and given up. There's a Chinese proverb that says, "Without forgiveness, you may as well dig two graves—one for the person who has harmed you and one for yourself." I agree with this. Holding anger in your heart will only make your life one of unhappiness, and forgiveness is a gift you give yourself every single day. I have forgiven my rapist, and it has let me live. But forgiveness does not begin to change what happened or to erase the memory of trauma, nor should it replace our country's justice system. We should forgive, but we shouldn't give up. We shouldn't stop fighting for justice when a crime has been committed, or fighting to prevent such crimes in the first place.

Campus sexual assaults continue, at my alma mater and elsewhere, though universities often try to keep such things quiet, to protect their endowment and the reputation of the university. Rape statistics have little place in the glossy brochures distributed to potential students and alumni donors. These institutions are more willing to cite a student for underage alcohol use than for the felony of rape. The University of Virginia has updated its sexual assault policy since I was a student. Shamim Sisson, a dean at UVA at the time it adopted the new policy, was quoted in the *Hook* as saying that serving on the Sexual Assault Board was "a great learning experience." But her comments made those of us who were trying to foster change at the university wonder exactly what lessons she had learned. She described the "real" problem as girls drinking so much at parties that they're not in control, and said that alcohol education was the key to ending sexual violence. Unfortunately, this is a way of blaming victims, and putting the burden on women to prevent such crimes. There was no suggestion that heavy-drinking, potentially violent male students should receive interventions.

It's a hard fact. One likes to think that if you go to one of the best universities in the country, filled with nice people from nice families, you will be safe and protected. But crimes do happen, and many universities are interested first and foremost in protecting themselves. When a college or university tells you, as they did me, "We are reviewing our policies," it sometimes means, "Please do sit down, be quiet, and eventually go away." When they say they've updated the policy, it means, "Look here—we're doing just enough to make you sit down, be quiet, and eventually go away." Question authority.

However, rape is not simply a university issue. Nor is it just a women's issue. Rape occurs every day, everywhere. It's a human rights issue and we all have a responsibility to take care of our friends, family, and children. To help them if it has happened. To listen and not judge. To assist in the healing. To open a dialogue and not shy away from the word "rape." We owe that to survivors.

In September 2008 I gave birth to my second child, a child I had been told not to hope for, because of my age and my history and all the stress my body had been through. Ava got a baby brother: Leonardo Michael Seccuro, born on a Sunday afternoon to the soundtrack of Bruce Springsteen's "Promised Land," with a full head of blond hair, perfect tiny hands, and gorgeous blue eyes. Several months later, in the summer of 2009, my newly expanded family left our beloved Greenwich and settled in Alexandria, Virginia. Here, I am closer to those who work for victims' rights on Capitol Hill. My own work as an advocate has just begun.

Shortly after Beebe's release, I found myself back in the Hamptons. While driving through Amagansett, I had the worst panic attack of my life. I made Mike pull over and rolled in the grass like a madwoman, gulping for air. An hour later, I wandered into the aptly named Equilibrium surf shop. I had surfed before, but had never had proper lessons. They gave me the name of a surfing instructor, and I called. We met the next morning for paddling practice at a lake and bonded immediately; I told him right off the bat that I was a survivor of sexual assault. I began to train with him regularly. He made me laugh and took no excuses from me on those cold early mornings. The horrible panic attack that day in the car would become my salvation. Soon, I graduated from the lake back to the ocean. Board slung under my newly muscled arm, wet suit stripped halfway down, I became a warrior. There is a moment when the ocean first rises up behind you and you can feel no past, no future, just the gorgeous reality of the present as you are lifted up, find your balance, and ride the wave. There is no better feeling.

Acknowledgments

To my wonderful agent, Kate Lee of ICM: You took a chance that people would want to know my story and you shepherded me with such humor and sheer intelligence. To my Los Angeles agent, Josie Freedman of ICM, your e-mails make me smile and I love our visits. You are the real deal.

To my amazing editors at Bloomsbury, Kathy Belden and Rachel Mannheimer: You were so patient with me and waited so long for this work while Leo was arriving into the world. Thank you for your talent, encouragement, and shaping of my very emotional words into a meaningful work.

To Lindsay: This is for you, because of you. Sending you the most love and true meaning of honor.

To S. Daniel Carter and Jonathan Kassa at the nonprofit Security on Campus, Inc.: Thank you for opening my eyes and beginning my education. You were my first mentors on this journey. You make schools safer for children and help parents to rest easy. I know we have much work to do. And I'm proud to do it with you.

To Connie and the late Howard Clery: I think of Jeanne every day. Know that I respect your quest and that her death was not in vain. Thank you for sharing your pain with the world so that others may learn.

To Scott and Tori, founders of RAINN, and the warriors who run the best organization—Kate, Rachel, Elizabeth: I thank you for being there and showing this nation the best in advocacy and care. You make every bit of difference for countless survivors.

To Dan and Gil Harrington: Meeting you has been terrible, under the circumstances, but a great gift as you fight your fight. You and your family, including the beloved, late Morgan, teach me lessons in grace and humility each day. 2-4-1.

To Susan Russell: Thank you for crusading and for letting me into the life of your family and into your struggle. You and Katherine have shown such grace in the face of such adversity.

To Cherri Murphy, my victim advocate: What would I have done without you—your easy laugh, your calming and empowering voice, your words of common sense, blessing, and wisdom, your willingness to give so easily of yourself when I needed a shoulder? I am proud to call you "friend."

To Claude Worrell: Your grace, intelligence, perseverance, and humor got me through eighteen months of trying times. You are such an asset to the people of Charlottesville and I hope they realize what they have in you. You worked endlessly with me and explained the convoluted system to us tirelessly. Please thank Kathryn and your children for us as well. You are like family to us. What you have done is change the face of what it means to be a rape victim. And you did it without fanfare in what became a media event. You also understood my need to speak out and be a voice for others. You are a true gentleman and I know you'll continue to fight this fight for me and for others.

To Detective Nicholas Rudman: You are like a brother to me. Never have I witnessed such amazing police work, such complete and utter dedication to finding the answers and finding justice for us. I really don't have the proper words to express my gratitude to you. You are a credit to the Charlottesville Police Department, the citizens of Charlottesville, and, of course, your family. I also wish to thank Sergeant Rick Hudson and Detectives Scott Godfrey and Bob Sclafani for their diligence and sense of honor.

To Chief Tim Longo: Simply put, you are my hero. Your legacy will be one of strength tempered with good sense, a steel will and a charming way. You took my call that December day and were the first to understand the gravity of what had taken place. You validated me and never once backed down. During the darkest days of this case, you picked up the phone and made the time to encourage me to stay with it. I wish you every good thing in life, as you are the embodiment of what an officer and a gentleman should be in this nation.

To Marnie Goodfriend, my fellow survivor and, of course, good friend: Thank you for being there always.

To my sorority sisters, friends, and fellow survivors: Bret, Shannon, Kris B., Sharan, Sally, Tiffany, Kris D., Shari, Donna, Kris K., Christianne, Lisa D., Trish, Anne, Pam K., Pam W., Tabatha and John, Lisa and Drew, Lee and Elee, Les and Kathryn, Courteney, Nathalie, Lisa G., Erin, Mario, Michele, Tamara and Andrew, Patty, Jules, Anne, Annie H., Kristin, Claire, and, of course, Big Al: Your support, both physical and electronic, was so meaningful. It's as if twenty years have not passed. You are all so wonderful and I am blessed to call you sisters and brothers.

To Peter, my therapist: Thank you for our years working together and for putting me back together. You are a miracle worker.

To Tony Caramanico: Thanks for getting me back on the board and getting my head straight. You had more to do with my healing than you will ever know.

To my wonderful in-laws, Pat and Steve Mead: Thanks for being such a great help and support during this time. You've made this transition for your grandchildren so easy. Know how much you are loved and respected.

To Mom and Dad: This is for you—it sets right how you were wronged. Know how much I love you. Know that you did everything you could. Know that it finally worked out.

To Mike: It was never up to you to fix what was broken. The sacrifices you made for our family showed how much you cared without your saying a word. The love you give to me and our children speaks volumes and I am lucky to have found you.

To my little ones: May you grow up in a safer world, one that Mama can help make so for you. You are everything good and beautiful and innocent and I want you to know that I love you both like the moon, the stars, and the sun.

And to all the survivors who've written: You know who you are. I kept your names on a list while I wrote this. I am so sorry that the list is so very long. But you will be fine. Better than fine. You will find peace.

A Note on the Author

Liz Seccuro is an event planner and victims' rights activist. She lives in Alexandria, Virginia, with her family. This is her first book. Follow her on Twitter @CrashIntoMeBook.